DEMYSTIFLYING

DEMYSTIFLYING

How to Become a Pilot for Those Who Don't Speak Pilot

Kine A. Paulsen

>

**INSPIRATION
BY THE COAST**
los angeles

Inspiration by the Coast

www.inspirationbythecoast.com

Published in the United States by Inspiration by the Coast
Publishing

For information about special discounts for bulk purchases, please
contact Inspiration by the Coast at hi@inspirationbythecoast.com

Library of Congress Cataloging-in-Publication Data is available.

ISBN: 0-578-39409-X
ISBN-13: 978-0-578-39409-1

Illustrations: Vanessa Robaina
Photo credit: Peter Bakema, PHCS R. L. Lawson, U.S. Air Force
Master Sgt. David Richards
Cover Design: KAP
Edited by Kind Souls

CONTENTS

CONTENTS

To my co-pilot, Cali

Introduction

IT WAS DURING A MENTOR dinner in college I got asked: if you had all the money in the world, what would you do? Without hesitation, I answered, I would get my pilot license so I could fly around the world. As luck would have it, I would start the process of getting a pilot license before I had "all the money in the world", but not without some challenges.

What do I do when faced with a challenge? I research. I obsess to find the answers, obsess to understand on my own terms. I wanted to read a book that would make stepping into the cockpit a little less overwhelming, a book that would simply explain the process, the ups and downs, and easy explanations without having to know how to speak "pilot" before even getting started. I looked all over, but when I couldn't find that book, I decided to write my own.

I was flustered, nervous, and completely new to this world when I started out. And wondered if I was the only one who had felt that way. Although you won't be a pilot by the end of this book, hopefully, you will be better prepared for the first step in that direction. If you show up only one percent less nervous because of a piece of information, I will be ecstatic. My journey of getting my pilot license is still ongoing, but I want to share what I have learned along the way.

I found that going online and looking for an entry ticket into the world of flying came with even more confusing jargon. I was inspired to write this book to inspire others to pursue their pilot license. By interviewing pilots around the world, from all walks of life, I hope to show you that you can become a pilot too. There is no prior knowledge or interest required. And you don't have to look a certain way or be a specific age for that matter.

Ask a pilot how to become a pilot, and you will most likely find yourself in an amazingly passionate, helpful conversation. But if you are like me, not a pilot and brand new to the world of aviation, it will probably leave you more confused. For every question, I find myself bursting to ask 15 additional questions. Somehow it feels intimidating to ask for a clarification when you don't understand 75% of the jargon spoken.

Pilots talk with an incredible passion in a different language. C172, Piper Cub, F-16, Niner, Zulu, knots, pitch and yaw, and altitude in feet. And "Oh my, you should've heard what ATC said the other day". Confused yet? Don't be, we will go over it all step by step together in the following chapters. The craft of piloting an aircraft is hard, but my wish with this book is to demystify flying. Or what I have come to call *demystiflying*.

This book is for you who are considering pursuing your pilot license, who might be curious what it is like to be a pilot or you may have already logged some hours. Or it may be a gift to someone you know, who has talked about getting into the cockpit, but are not sure where to start. If you already are a pilot, it might be fun to reflect on how much you had to learn in order to get to where you are today. This book is not meant to replace any educational tools, but meant as motivation and inspiration and to teach you to speak basic pilot.

In this book, we'll start of with some benefits and challenges of becoming a pilot, go through the many paths and cost to getting your license, and some basic flight knowledge. In addition you will get a *very* brief, but inspiring, lesson in aviation history and learrn some basics on how to spot different aircraft.

In all the interviews I conducted and numerous books and articles I read, one thing is for sure: It requires motivation, determination, and humbleness to become a pilot. But my hope is that this book will make the journey from your couch to the cockpit a little easier. In writing this book, I have interviewed 200 pilots from all over the world. It is hard to come by a more helpful crowd than pilots, they genuinely want to spread their experience in the skies.

Lastly, I hope you enjoy this book, and I would love your thoughts on it, either in a review or by emailing me directly at hi@demystiflying.com. I would also love to hear your #demystiflying stories, or if you have any questions, don't be a stranger.

Blue skies and happy landings,
Kine
Los Angeles - 2022

CHAPTER ONE

Blue skies, grey skies

FLYING IS A MAGICAL THING. However, just like in life, there will be days with blue skies and days with grey skies. I could absolutely be referring to the weather conditions with that statement, but in this case, I'm referring to it metaphorically. Blue skies are those days that everything will feel easy and joyful. Grey skies are those days where you might encounter challenges that will make you question if you're even cut out for flying. Before embarking on the road to becoming a master of the skies, let's go over the benefits and downsides of becoming a pilot.

Blue skies

BEYOND BEING KNOWN AS THE pilot amongst your friends or being able to nonchalantly say "yeah, I fly airplanes" at a dinner party, what are some of the rewards of getting your pilot license? So what are some perks of getting your license:

Freedom

"Once you have tasted flight, you will forever walk the earth with your eyes turned skyward, for there you have been, and there you will always long to return" — Leonardo da Vinci, Italian polymath during the High Renaissance

Think back to that first time you drove a car after you got your license. Personally, I drove straight to a nearby fast food joint to buy burgers for my friends. I remember that overwhelming feeling that the world was mine. I could go everywhere. If I could learn to drive a car, what could I accomplish next? (I also managed to kill the engine on a red light when waving at my friend's dad due to stick shift troubles, but that's beside the point.) The freedom was real. It was the beginning of an adventure. I still love driving. But I have come to learn that I'm not alone on the streets, especially not in Los Angeles, where I currently reside. If only I could get around faster without being stopped by traffic. Cue airplanes.

That feeling of freedom is multiplied, exponentially, by being up in the skies. You're not constrained by roads but can make your own (sort of). With the right plan and resources, you can really go anywhere your heart desires. And faster than by car. Imagine seeing some of the world's most beautiful places from the air. But also landing in remote spots that you wouldn't get by foot or by car.

This perk of ultimate freedom was a repeated topic in my interviews. Mike Krass, the curious entrepreneur turned pilot located in New Orleans, told me: "I continue to fly because any place that is further than 3 hours away will inevitably be faster and more fun to fly to than to drive there!" Or as long-time pilot Roger Noble enthusiastically shared with me: "Your local area becomes smaller. You can fly over the freeways during rush hour." Andy Christopher, U.S. Navy Reserve pilot, shares the same sentiment, "There is just that pure joy of flying". Even though Christopher is no longer active duty military, he feels grateful that he still gets paid to fly frequently in the reserves.

There is an enormous sense of freedom knowing that if you wanted to you could eat lunch in a different city and be home for dinner. Or that you have the opportunity to offer to pick something or someone up from a completely different area in a time of need. You can be that person.

A craft that will take a lifetime to master

"One of the things I teach my children is that I have always invested in myself, and I have never stopped learning, never stopped growing" — Chesley Sullenberger, airline captain of infamous US Airways Flight 1549 that landed in the Hudson River in New York

Most pilots would say that the day you think you've accomplished everything as a pilot, you are overconfident and shouldn't be flying anymore. This opportunity to always be a student is something that so many pilots talk so fondly about. There is always a new skill or aircraft to learn. No matter what type of aircraft you start flying in, there will always be new challenges to face. Even without learning anything new, most pilots are still trying to improve their techniques and procedures whenever they get into the cockpit.

This never-ending journey to get the perfect flight was often mentioned in my interviews. Randy Brooks, Vice President at Aviation Performance Solutions and pilot of many years will proudly admit he has never had a perfect flight. "I've had close to perfect flights, but never a perfect flight. A perfect flight isn't possible." Experienced pilots like Brooks will agree: There is always something you can improve, whether it is the take-off, the flying, or the landing or all the many things in between. Some would say the day they land feeling they've had a perfect flight, will be the day they quit. Like so many other things in life, but especially true in aviation, safety and overconfidence go together like olive oil and water.

Another seeker of continuous learning is California-based serial entrepreneur and hobby pilot, Gary Paquette. Even though he started taking lessons in 1976, he is about to embark on another challenge in his training through loss of control, so-called upset classes. Simply explained these classes are designed training environments that put the pilot out of control of aircraft and will teach him to recover in an emergency situation. Paquette has throughout his pilot journey consistently taken classes to become a better, but more importantly, safer pilot.

A good pilot is often characterized as someone who is self-aware of when he or she needs more training. There are required hours to get your license and additional hours required to stay current with your license once you get it, but a good pilot will know when he or she needs to spend some

8

extra time getting familiar with flying again. If you love learning, you'll love that aspect of flying. There is always going to be a new learning opportunity. There are always going to be new certifications, new aircraft, and of course, new destinations. Becoming a pilot you will have a craft that will take a lifetime to master.

The real airplane mode

"I fly because it releases my mind from the tyranny of petty things"
– Antoine de Saint-Exupery, author and aviator

From the early days of aviation, pilots have discussed being in the zone. Being in the cockpit means a complete focus on flying the plane. In many of my interviews, the way pilots spoke of the act of flying could easily be mistaken for meditation. Not in the form of breathing exercises or mindfulness, but because there are so many moving elements as part of flying. From preparation, take off, flying, and landing, you have to be present in that very moment.

Unlike being forced to switch to airplane mode during a flight and leaving everything in the hand of the airline crew, this kind of airplane mode has a new meaning. As soon as you get to the airfield, you'll enter a natural airplane mode. Whether you are a hobby pilot or a professional pilot, you have to give the airplane your full attention. Without your full attention, accidents are more likely to happen.

A number of the pilots I spoke to explained being in control of an aircraft is a way to get into the state of flow. In the book *Flow: The Psychology of Optimal Experience*, psychologist Mihaly Csikszentmihalyi, describes the state of flow as "joy, creativity, the process of total involvement with life". Csikszentmihalyi studied the subject of flow over years to discover that this feeling of happiness does not necessarily come without working for it. Through his research, he discovered that these moments that we sometimes remember years after are the ones we had to work a little extra for. A pilot in the training flying solo for the first time or a seasoned pilot flying into a new airport many years later often embodied Csikszentmihalyi's findings. As the psychologist writes in his global bestseller: "The best moments usually occur when a person's body or mind is stretched to its limits in a voluntary effort to accomplish something difficult or worthwhile."

Louise Heap, UK-based former Royal Air Force pilot and Head of Aerospace at Air Race, wrote the following about this sense of flow after many years of hiatus from flying a C-130. C-130, aka the Hercules, is a massive airplane that can carry almost three and. a half times the weight of an elephant.:

"Flying always made me feel a sense of freedom. From the first flight I took with my military instructor, that sense of weightlessness as we lifted off the ground, to the operational sorties I flew as a C-130J pilot, the exhilaration and thrill of speeding down the runway to lift off, never left me. It's a sense of being untouchable - like you're speeding down the runway and leaving everything behind; to escape the mundane norms of the world, to get away from the negativities, or literally, to escape a war and rescue injured soldiers; that moment of liftoff and the subsequent climb through the air to a "safe height" achieved peace and quiet like I don't think I have experienced since. You could be on a packed aircraft, with a full crew and other passengers on the flight deck, having just left a sandstorm or a firefight, but that moment you reach height and level off, the panic and chaos were gone and the world was peaceful. I loved the exhilaration of taking off and landing, but that immediate sense of calm as the aircraft leveled off and all checks were complete is something I cannot replicate on the ground. It was a moment to breathe, to take it all in and just "be". I miss the level-off."

Being in the zone and focusing on being the best possible pilot actually turns out to be a perk. No matter what kind of challenges you are facing on the ground, you will be forced to shift focus while in the air. This airplane mode gives your brain a break from the things you may be facing down on the earth plane. Since there are always new challenges to tackle as a pilot, there will always be opportunities to chase that airplane mode.

A sense of accomplishment

"Every worthwhile accomplishment, big or little, has its stages of drudgery and triumph, a beginning, a struggle, and a victory" - Mahatma Gandhi, Indian activist

Starting your pilot journey, you'll most likely feel overwhelmed. You'll probably doubt your ability to get to the day where you master the clouds on your own. If not, you'll be one of the first pilots who haven't. Common for all the pilots I spoke to, is that everyone shared a story (or many) of doubting their ability to become a pilot at some point. But at the other end of that doubt, they would speak of a sense of accomplishment. From the first lesson to the first solo to getting a license in hand, there is a lot of thrilling milestones. The excitement to hear pilots recount these moments was contagious.

According to research done in 2011 by Aircraft Owners and Pilot Association (AOPA), the largest aviation association in the world, only 30% of students who sign up for flight lessons will get their license. We can't shy away from the fact that becoming a pilot is not a walk in the park, but it better explains the sense of accomplishment. Being able to finish something that so many others have quit before you, is a great feeling. You did it. Despite the odds.

Knight Campbell, a retired U.S. Navy helicopter pilot based in San Diego, told me "I wanted to become a pilot because I watched Top Gun growing up, and thought it was this impossible thing." For Campbell, it was the thrill of achieving the unachievable that kept him going when he faced tough times.

Tammy Barlette, a retired U.S. Air Force fighter pilot, found herself the odd one out when she started flight training. Being surrounded by a group of engineers and peers who had dreamed of becoming a pilot from an early age, she wasn't sure she belonged at first. "I didn't think I fit in the group, but I knew they had selected me for this opportunity for a reason. That they thought I was equipped to take on this challenge." Barlette stuck with it and went on to become an accomplished fighter pilot and instructor pilot in the military for over 20 years. Here are some inspiring thoughts from different pilots on describing their moments of accomplishments:

- "Flying did not come to me at first, but it seemed to come all of a sudden and then it came big." - Lincoln Beachey, early aviation pioneer and world record holder

- "My first solo felt like 2 days, but in reality, was only 10 minutes. I was initially really nervous, but then I decided to do what I had to trust what I had learned, and just enjoy it." - Jan Slangen, author and former Frecce Tricolori pilot

- "I DID THAT! Something I will never forget. I think the first solo was followed by two flights later that day. I wanted to go up again, again and again. Could not get

enough. Learning to fly is not a natural thing, but it is
one of the most rewarding things I feel almost anyone
can accomplish." - Jim Anderson, Vice President at
Starr Aviation and long-time pilot

And there are so many stories like these. They all share the
same conclusion: the benefit of sticking to the course and an
overwhelming sense of achievement.

A community of like-minded individuals

*"Friendship is born at that moment when one person says to
another: 'What! You too? I thought I was the only one."* — C.S.
Lewis, British writer

Many of us have met new friends through new hobbies. And
often it is easier to create a new bond with someone who
shares a common interest. It gives a chance to skip the
awkward small talk and start a conversation on common
ground. The pilot world is no different. One of the major
benefits of becoming a pilot is the new world of potential
friendships it brings.

Lifelong friendships were built among pilots from all
walks of life. Young, aspiring pilots who met at the local
airport. Military officers bonding over the grueling flight
training. Commercial airline pilots who have become friends
through the ups and downs of working in the airline
industry. So many have shared stories of this incredible
camaraderie amongst pilots.

As the adage goes that the best friendships are built in the
trenches, which was an ongoing theme in my conversations.
Especially pilots who got their training in the military and
aviation colleges spoke about those moments that happened
after both good and bad days in the cockpit. "I have never
experienced that kind of camaraderie before or after flight
school. It was a hyper-competitive environment, but we also

supported each other through thick and thin. We were all so focused on the same goal: becoming pilots," recounted retired U.S. Marine Corps pilot, Bryan E. Miller, out of Los Angeles.

This support is found between people across all levels and ages, not just between peers. New pilots get helped along in their training by more experienced pilots or the other way around when it came to new technology. Most pilots want to see other aspiring pilots succeed and will often lend a hand or even a flight.

And the friendliness of the aviation community is real. I was blown away by the helpfulness I received when embarking on this adventure of learning how to fly and also writing this book. I got only a handful of rejections in requests for interviews. And those few no's I received were due to scheduling issues. People would give up whole chunks of their time to a complete stranger who was writing a book to invite others into the ranks of aviation.

The community of pilots can be compared to an exclusive club where new members are always welcome. Pilots love to share stories about their experiences. Yes, they will often use jargon, but that's because once you enter that cockpit it's like you've stepped into a different country. It can be compared to learning a new language. One that you'll learn to speak as you started traveling into that world. With a new set of friends!

Unexpected adventures

"The purpose of life, after all, is to live it; to taste experience to the utmost, to reach out eagerly and without fear for newer and richer experiences." - Eleanor Roosevelt, American political figure

When getting your pilot license, not only will you learn to fly, but you'll also find that you'll stumble on unexpected adventures. Adventures in terms of experiences, but also new areas of interest. When I took my first flight lesson, I never imagined that I would learn so much about history, geography, culture, aerodynamics, leadership, mindset, and beyond.

Friends would introduce me to other people they knew who were pilots. I got invited to the Warner Bros. Pictures hangars to see the private jets they own (so LA I know!). And an acquaintance I made waiting at an airport gate turned into me getting to experience a Gulfstream G5 simulator (Gulfstreams are known for being rapped about as a private jet for the rich and famous). None of these were events that would have happened if I hadn't taken that one lesson. Here are some of my favorite stories of unexpected adventures that happened from learning how to fly:

- Alexander Trent was studying business in San Francisco when he asked a friend of his sister who was an instructor if he could have a lesson with her. That one lesson changed his career aspiration completely to where he ended up moving to Arizona to become an airline pilot and today works full-time in the skies.
- Lorraine M. Herr went to take lessons to become a private pilot and ended up marrying her instructor. Today she and her husband live close to a small airport outside Chicago and enjoy watching their son continue the family tradition of flying.
- Bjørn Kjos saw a fighter pilot fly over his small village growing up which inspired him to join the Norwegian Air Force. After many years in the cockpit, he changed gears and became a lawyer. Years later he changed gears again and founded Norwegian Airlines, which over the years became a global company with over 100 routes and the fourth-largest low-cost airline in Europe.

Once you open that door to that cockpit, you are inviting in new opportunities.

You already have some applicable skills

"The future belongs to those who learn more skills and combine them in creative ways" — Robert Greene, American author

Many pilots reflecting on their initial training had a common wish to go back in time and accept the feeling of not knowing it all from the beginning. They said they would have welcomed celebrating small wins despite being overwhelmed by the process. Even if they didn't have the confidence in their flying abilities yet, they would have welcomed the confidence that they were exactly where they were supposed to be in their training.

Many new students try to make sense of it all and strive for this impossible perfection already in the first lesson. I'm here to tell you, you might as well accept that you'll never learn everything there is to know. Better use of your energy is accepting that one of the amazing perks of flying is that you'll have access to a life-lasting college. "You're always going to learn new elements of flying," says Canadian airline pilot David Culos. He regularly seeks out new challenges in aviation to go back to the feeling of his initial training. Further educating yourself and continuing to learn the craft will keep you on your toes for a lifetime.

Sometimes we forget how much it requires to learn a new skill. If you learned how to bike or swim, you know it didn't happen automatically. A good approach when starting is to create a list of skills you already possess that may be useful to flying. Maybe you're good at making checklists. Maybe you're a surfer and know how to read weather reports. Maybe you're good at reading maps. Or you're interested in car engines? I promise you, you're not coming into this world without any prior skills that aren't applicable. And building on skills you already have can make the process more fun.

Grey skies

THE REWARDS AND MEMORIES ONE gets from being a pilot are endless. However, there are some challenges you'll have to face as well:

Levelsetting

"Fly. Just do it. Most people will find a million excuses not to: it's inconvenient, it's confusing, flight instructors quit. There will be plenty of excuses, but sticking to the course is worth it. There is nothing like flying"— Bob Pittman, founder of MTV and iheartradio.com

Most of us have at some point looked up in the sky and daydreamed of flying an airplane or helicopter. But there might be a gap between reality and dreams. "There really should be some level setting to what flying really is. There is an expectation that flying is this whimsical, fairy-tale experience. You're a bird in the skies. Flying is not that. Flying is an individual discipline." says Brian E. Miller, retired U.S. Marine Corps pilot, "It wasn't until I had flown a few hundred hours before the magic happened for me. That was when I had the available mind space to take it all in. Gosh, I get emotional talking about it. Flying for me is spiritual. It's pure magic."

Miller believes everyone can get to that point. All that requires is taking the time and energy and they will get there too. He further admits that it might take fewer hours for someone who does their flight training outside the military.

He started his training in a military trainer plane, which in comparison to a standard trainer plane at your local flight school, goes a lot faster and is more complex to operate.

For others that magical feeling came a lot sooner in their training. Some fell in love with flying during their first lessons, but for many, it took a little longer. The key is to not try to solve at what level you enjoy flying in the first few lessons. Flying can be overwhelming, yet it can be one of the more rewarding skills you'll ever learn. You can decide flying is not for you, but you can also at any point change your mind again. There are plenty of examples of people who changed their minds or took a few breaks in their training.

One pilot I spoke to did not enjoy that first flight at all. "The instructor was rude and hated his job. I left thinking I would never fly again", she explained. Chance had it that she got to experience a second flight with a better instructor and she fell in love with flying. She went on to become a professional pilot. She now looks back at a successful career as a long-time airline pilot with one of the largest airlines in the world.

The actor Morgan Freeman originally joined the U.S. Air Force to become a pilot. But when he finally sat in the cockpit for the first time, the experience didn't match his childhood dreams. Once in an interview Freeman said: "I had this very clear epiphany. You are not in love with this. You are in love with the idea of this." Years later, he sat in the cockpit while out flying with his business partner, who was a private pilot. At some point during the flight he asked Freeman to take the controls. Right there, at that moment, he decided to get his license. Which he did, and he got it within only four months of that flight.

Another famous actor, Harrison Ford, took a major break in his flight training. He started taking lessons in the 1960s but was forced to stop because it was too expensive. Over the following years, Ford went on to become a successful movie star and though he had the funds it took a long time for him to get back into the cockpit. Thirty years later he bought a plane and started flying again, and officially got his license at age 53.

A lot of people will hear that learning to fly can be challenging and that it will take some additional time to get really good at it as a way to excuse themselves from pursuing a pilot license. If that is you, here is my advice: give yourself permission to take one introductory flight. This is also often referred to as a discovery flight, which is a short flight designed to familiarize you with what it entails to fly an airplane.

Think of your introductory flight as a first date without any further commitment. If you fall in love on the first date, great! If you don't, you might want to take a second or third lesson (and maybe see other instructors), but no one is forcing you to get married aka become a pilot. Later in the book, we'll discuss ways to make this introductory flight the best possible experience.

Learning Challenges

"When everything seems to be against you, remember that an airplane takes off against the wind, not with it" — Henry Ford, American automobile manufacturer

Even though I often heard about "the natural pilot", that pilot who never struggled in his or her pilot training, I have yet to meet. The greater majority of the pilots I spoke to had one or many moments in learning how to fly. While some struggle more with the act of flying, other students struggle more with the theoretical portion, and some admitted to struggling with the whole process. This made me think: like in regular life, maybe from the outside it might appear that someone has it all figured out? While in reality, they most likely have their own areas they're hoping to improve?

One pilot told me, despite years of reading aviation magazines and spending hours at the airport, the first lesson he had he felt "like an idiot." Others shared how they had questioned one or many times if they would ever be able to fly. Ryan Casey, explained over the phone one day from Wilmington, the importance of acknowledging that as a pilot you are always going to be a student. "The sooner you can get to "I'm going to suck", the better your journey will be", he said, reflecting over his career as a helicopter pilot in the U.S. Marine Corps.

This notion was echoed by so many I spoke to. Kim "KC" Campbell, an accomplished U.S. Air Force pilot, is someone who's had to learn complex airplane systems in different cockpits over the years. She shared a plan of action on how to combat the expected mistakes you are bound to make: "You need to realize you are going to make mistakes. Once they happen, you make note of what those are and commit to not repeat those in the future."

I often heard that in order to withstand the challenging journey of getting your license, you'll need to already be passionate about aviation. If you're like me, that might make you feel a little defeated. I always dreamt of flying, but never really had a strong interest in the world of aviation. For me, my interest grew over time as I learned more and became more confident in my own knowledge.

I was relieved when many of the pilots I interviewed had no prior interest, knowledge, or experience when they got started. "I was surrounded by people who already knew a lot more than me, they made it look so natural. It was harder for me, but that only meant I had to put in the extra effort," United Airlines pilot Jessica Wolcott said. Today she is happy that the beginning stage was challenging because the extra effort has made her a better pilot.

Former fighter pilot, Tammy Barlette, had a similar experience. She joined the U.S. Air Force after a chance encounter in college. The moment of doubt was real the first day she drove on to Laughlin Air Force base in Texas. "I remember driving to base and seeing two airplanes flying in formation and landing at the same time, thinking to myself "There is no way I'll ever be able to do that"". When others might have turned around and given in to their inner voices, Barlette decided there and then to change her focus.

Instead of focusing on her current inability to fly jets in formation, she decided that her immediate goal was to park her car and find the room where she would be living for the remainder of her time at Laughlin. Slowly, but surely, over her time in training, she would mentally set new, slightly bigger goals. Barlette would always build on her confidence in completing the micro-goals until one day she was that pilot taking off in a fighter jet doing formations.

Being patient when facing learning challenges has been spoken about since the early days of aviation. Glen Curtiss, one of the early pioneers in flying, wrote about the importance of taking the time it requires in his book *The Curtiss Aviation Book*, written in 1912. Granted he was willing to take greater risks than we will ever have to face with a modern airplane. Curtiss flew a self-built airplane with no cockpit just sitting attached to the wings.

But he echoes what so many pilots still say today: leave behind the idea of mastering how to fly an aircraft without trial and error. In his book, he wrote: "Any man who wants to fly badly enough can fly." By going at your own pace and not comparing yourself to others, your ability and confidence will appear gradually. I had many similar conversations with pilots around the world, and they all lit up talking about why living through the challenges of learning was worth it.

You are going to get tired, very tired
"If you get tired, learn to rest, not quit" - Unknown

Anyone who's learned a new language or skill can attest to getting exhausted from all the learning that takes place. A quick trip on Google will uncover thousands of searches from language students around the world wondering if they're the only ones getting really tired from speaking a foreign language. Personally, I have never been as tired as I was when I was learning Spanish in my adult years. Research conducted by the University of Copenhagen also backs this up: when you concentrate really hard on a task, such as trying to master a language, your body will get fatigued and produce serotonin to prevent our bodies from becoming hyperactive. In other words, your brain will tell you you need to be tired.

Now imagine learning a million new buttons, hand, and feet coordination, a new language (radio communication), and the ability to evaluate situations before they happen - all at the same time. "Yes, you get exhausted. You're using parts of your brain at a different level than you have before. And that can actually translate to physical exhaustion" says Sharon Preszler, a retired Southwest Airlines pilot. She adds, "But remember it's a step by step process, the learning is designed to be in building blocks."

There will be hundreds of things to learn when you get your training, but if you're not the type of person who likes serious commitment to new skills, this might not be for you. But like learning a new language, starting a new company, or riding a bike, staying the course will be worth it. Sometimes that means taking a smaller break or learning a concept from another perspective in the forms of a new instructor or another educational source.

Money

"To make a small fortune in aviation, start with a big one!" - old adage in aviation

One pilot I spoke to grew up fascinated by airplanes. His grandfather would take him to a local airport to entertain him at a young age, but he knew early on that his parents wouldn't be able to financially support his dream. If he was to fulfill his dream, he would have to figure it out on his own. He went all over town looking for jobs and eventually stumbled into a local radio station where he got a job to fund his license.

Not only did this translate to a more comfortable voice on the radio in the cockpit, but this was also the start of what became his career in media. The person I spoke to is Bob Pittman, former CEO of AOL and co-founder of MTV and iHeartRadio. It's an incredible reminder that by creatively solving one problem in life, we welcome other opportunities. He could've let the lack of financial resources stop him, but he didn't.

If becoming a pilot was cheaper, more people would probably do it. Not taking into account a college degree or going through the military as options, on average it is estimated that a license at a local flight school will cost in the range of $6,000 to $20,000. The price varies depending on what kind of aircraft you want to fly (helicopter vs. airplane and what kind of model you rent for your lessons), what your flight instructor charges, and also your learning pace.

You should expect a higher price in bigger cities, like Los Angeles and New York City. Like other things in life, if it seems too good to be true, it probably is. But the price to entry is high also makes the clouds more magically grand. And with less traffic than you'll find on roads. Later in the book, you'll find a whole chapter dedicated to breaking down the costs and solving the financial challenge.

Time

"The best pilots fly more than the others; that's why they're the best" - Chuck Yeager, the first pilot to fly faster than the speed of sound

Due to country-specific differences in laws and regulations, the pilot license requirements I list in this book might vary depending on where you are located. However, the path to getting your license is typically very similar to the one in the U.S. How long does it take to become a pilot? For simplicity's sake, let's take a look at the most common starter license for new pilots, the private pilot license.

When you get the private pilot license you will be able to fly on your own and you can transport passengers. To qualify for the private pilot license the Federal Aviation Association (FAA), the department that regulates all aspects of civil aviation in the U.S., requires 40 hours in flight, a medical certificate, a written exam, and a final check ride. We'll go over this more in detail in a later chapter. However, most people end up spending more than the required hours.

Here are some common reasons people end up spending more time getting their license:

1. Safety is number one when it comes to flying. It is extremely important that you display confidence in all elements that both your instructor and FAA expect of you. Getting to that level of confidence can sometimes take longer.

2. Life gets in the way. Finances, changing work schedules, flight school cancellations. Missing a flight lesson is not like missing a workout.

3. Weather. As a student pilot, you are bound to be a

victim of the weather gods as bad weather can cancel your lessons last minute. For that reason, Arizona and Florida are flight school havens!

4. The vast amount of knowledge. Unless you've been immersed in the world of aviation from a young age, the amount of knowledge you are expected to learn in only 40 hours is overwhelming. Take the time you need to really understand.

Many flight instructors recommend flying at least two to three times a week, which many find to be a challenge. If you are worried about fitting flying lessons into a busy work week, one way to solve this is to get up really early and schedule your flying lessons in the morning. In many places, you can take advantage of statistically better weather conditions by doing so. Another solution is to commit to flying a lot in a shorter period of time.

But what if you travel a lot for work? So was Michael Govan, director of the Los Angeles Contemporary Museum of Art (LACMA), when he was encouraged by his friend, artist James Turrell, to start flying. Govan was at the time extremely busy traveling frequently and had no idea how he would juggle flying lessons and his intense work and travel. Turrell was insistent and would call Govan often to ask if he started his lessons yet. Eventually, Govan was convinced and found a creative solution: when he traveled in the U.S. he scheduled lessons at local airports in the cities he visited. He told me, in the end, that it made him a more well-rounded pilot learning in different airports with different instructors.

The path to your pilot's license may take you more or less time than someone else's. But it is better to spend extra time (and the money) to learn properly and fly with confidence. Note - if a school tells you you can do it remarkably quick, consider it a red flag!

Letting nerves get in the way

"In any given moment we have two options: to step forward into growth or step back into safety" Abraham Maslow, American physchologist

Some of the most seasoned pilots will admit to still feeling nervous before flying, but don't view that as negative or embarrassing. Better yet, many believe a healthy amount of nerves is good before a flight because it makes you more focused and alert. It also reminds the most experienced aviators of the importance of consistent training and preparation.

As mentioned earlier in this book, many accomplished pilots talk about the importance of gradually mastering skills to build confidence. Learning step by step is a way to build confidence and shake off those nerves in the cockpit. It is very often confidence that is that missing piece between someone who is scared versus someone who is nervous. Tammy Jo Shults is a Southwest airline captain who in 2018 landed Flight 1380 departing from New York en route to Dallas with an engine failure shortly after takeoff. Shults went from being a kid who struggled with crippling anxiety all through her childhood to later in life safely landing an aircraft with its 5 crew members and 144 passengers without her heart rate ever elevating. In her book *Nerves of Steel*, she partly credits her years being an Out of Control instructor in the U.S. Navy before joining Southwest. Out of Control classes are when military flight instructors intentionally puts an aircraft out of control to make the student pilot recover the situation.

If you're scared to try new things, flying might be the perfect challenge for you. You most definitely will get more comfortable trying new things when you learn to fly as getting your pilot license is a series of firsts. First lesson, first time with the controls, and of course the first time landing.

Just remember to take note of your progress and realize that firsts become seconds and thirds.

And this mental practice isn't just used in the beginning stages. In training to become a formation leader for the legendary aerobatic demonstration team of the Italian Air Force, Frecce Tricolori, Massimo Tammaro, shared a similar story. Despite his many years as a Frecce Tricolori wingman, his first day of training to become the leader of the ten plane formation, he started with just one plane next to him. After some time, he started training with two planes, then three, and gradually adding one all the way up to ten. Flying planes only 6.5 feet (2 meters) apart requires an enormous sense of trust amongst a team, but also in the leader. Learning by adding smaller blocks is the best way to instill this trust and get the nerves of both the formation leader and the team under control.

"To me, someone being nervous about going up in a small airplane for the first time with a flight instructor that they have just met is a sign of intellect," says Florida-based flight instructor Jamie Beckett. Being nervous due to being new to a situation or being underprepared for what lies ahead is natural. It would be strange to not be nervous because you're doing something for the first time. And this isn't just relevant to your first lesson but throughout your pilot journey. If your instructor believes you need more time to improve, trust that they are looking out for you. Don't let your nerves get in the way of going for it.

We'll cover more on how to combat these potential challenges in later chapters. Now that we have gone over some of the key benefits and challenges, you may be dying to continue learning or you may be a little intimidated. Regardless, I encourage you to keep reading. Before you do so, drink a glass of water. Hydration is key.

CHAPTER TWO

Chairfly and checklist

NO MATTER HOW MUCH PREPARATION or research you do ahead of getting into the cockpit, there is nothing that can truly prepare you for the real deal. But some mental preparation can't hurt. Especially if it's based on the experience of others, who have gotten their license and gone through the experience before you.

In this chapter, we will chair-fly your pilot training with your own checklists made for your particular scenario. Not sure what I just wrote there? Chair-flying and checklists are two terms you'll become an expert on after reading this book.

Chair-flying is a common technique used in flying, from beginner lessons all the way to 100 high-performing pilot team missions in the military. It's just what it sounds like. You sit in a chair and go through your flight mentally to plan your steps so that you better tackle any potential anomalies. At any point, when you're asked during this chapter to envision your ideal scenario, feel free to close your eyes, lean back, and visualize what that looks like for you. It will, like chair-flying in the pilot world, prepare you for the experience ahead.

No chair-flying experience is complete without a checklist

in hand. According to the book *Checklist Manifesto* by Atul Gawande, checklists were introduced to aviation after a tragic airplane accident in Ohio in 1935. The safety of flying improved drastically in the following years. Checklists are like your normal to-do lists except the same list every time. Before, after and during, pilots go through these checklists to help ensure that they are not solely relying on their own memory. Since you are navigating your own body and mind in becoming a pilot, you'll be making your own checklists in this chapter.

And just like pilots, who are planning for their next flight, know that plans can and will deviate. As Erika Armstrong writes in *A Chick in the Cockpit*: "{..} pilots visualize what takeoff is going to look like. They plan, anticipate, calculate, but events happen that no one could ever foresee". Every school, instructor, and area is different, so you'll have to fill in the blanks to make it relevant to you.

Why

Before you start chasing any big goal, it is important to ask yourself "why?". This is even more true for your pilot license. When you take on a big project you will ask yourself this question many times. When I set out to write this book, my "why" was to inspire myself and others to dare to dream that we too could become pilots.

That "why" kept me going when I had no desire to write or someone hinted that this book wasn't needed. This kind of faltering inspiration is part of life. It is not a secret that getting your license comes at the price of a university degree, not just in terms of financial resources, but also the time it takes to truly hone the skill. Even when you establish your purpose, you'll face moments of doubt or life events that change your direction. That doubt is guaranteed when you take on a big challenge, but the "why" will be there to push you through those tough moments. There is no right or wrong answer to what your "why" is, but without it, it will be harder to stick to the training when things get tough.

As you'll come to learn from stories in this book, flying is both challenging and rewarding. Like any other situation where we try to learn a new skill, most of us will plateau in our training at some point, and knowing "why" will help us move past that point. Austrian psychiatrist, Victor Frankl once wrote "Once you know your "why", you can survive almost any how ", which rings true for aviation

Another reason why your purpose is so important, as suggested in an email from Danish pilot Alf Døj, is that you can align your resources with your goal. "Flying is not free and if you "just" want to fly for fun – you can get the proper certificate for that." There are different levels of certifications and requirements for the size of aircraft and how many passengers you are able to transport. Some will require more time, money, and additional sacrifices than others.

This "why" might be unclear if you've never stepped into a cockpit or if reading this book is your first step into the aviation world. For some, it might be taking their parents flying up the California coast, while for others it might be proving to themselves that they can do the seemingly impossible. Or maybe you recently watched the original (or the newest) Top Gun and can't shake off that dream of being behind the controls of a fighter jet.

One of my dear friends wrote me a note while this book was in infancy: "The best advice you can give to new students is listening to yourself when you start flying – most do not like it – this isn't something you have to do. Don't keep at it because it's "cool to be a pilot" or "I started it, so I am going to finish it." Traditional goals don't always make sense in flying. Knowing your "why" can therefore help you both on staying the course, but also know if it's your time to take a break or not continue. Your "why" is YOUR North Star, not anyone else's.

For many of the pilots, the "why" was defined from an early age. Whether it was through family members who were pilots, daydreaming in high school, or having been to a flight show, there was no doubt they wanted to become a pilot. But in many cases, that was also not the case:

- Jessica Cox was born without arms as a result of a rare birth defect. Though she had dreamt of flying through the clouds growing up, she had grown fearful of flying in her adult years. One day she had the opportunity to go up in a small airplane, which is when she decided to turn her fears into a challenge she was going to overcome. Cox eventually became the world's first licensed armless pilot. When we spoke she shared details of the plane she is currently building which will be the first exclusively foot-controlled airplane in history.

- Paige E. Rose was a Division 1 softball athlete at George Washington University when she was approached by a military recruiter. Without any prior interest in flying, she took the leap and joined the U.S. Marine Corps. Today, she flies CH-53E Super Stallion in San Diego and beyond (translation: a hell of a big and complicated helicopter).

- Massimo Tammaro was towards the end of his high school years when he saw a picture of a F-18 on a magazine cover. Little did he know how that moment would be the beginning of a highly accomplished aviation career. Having grown up in a small Italian coastal town he wasn't raised amongst pilots, but through determination and discipline, Tammaro became commander of the world's only acrobatic display squadron with ten airplanes, Frecce Tricolori.

I wish I could share all the incredible stories I was so fortunate to hear in this book. It is heartwarming to hear about friendships, relationships, careers, and adventures that all had one thing in common: starting on the pilot license adventure. Next let us explore how you can start yours.

Finding the right aircraft

First, let's start off with what kind of aircraft you will want to fly. Throughout history, there have been many types of aircraft: from wings (!) to hot air balloons and so on. Later on, I have dedicated a whole chapter to the history of aviation as well as a chapter on how to spot different kinds of aircraft. But in this chapter, we'll focus on helicopters and airplanes. With that said, if you decide to go ahead and pursue a career as an astronaut after reading this book, I'm totally taking credit.

A lot of people assume flying a helicopter and airplane are similar, but they are actually very different. There is certainly knowledge that you can use for either route, but the way they are operated is in big contrast to each other.

Here is my first warning: In the world of flying, pilots will most likely ask you if you fly rotary (helicopter) or fixed-wing (airplane). To complicate matters a little pilots do not say they have their helicopter or airplane license, they will refer to a helicopter license as a rotary rating and an airplane license as a fixed-wing rating. And if you run into a pilot who can fly both types, they will say they are dual-rated. There are different models and types of each. There are also hybrids, meaning airplanes that take off and land like helicopters. In this book, I'll continue to refer to them as helicopters and airplanes.

For simplicity, I've made a broad overview comparing the features and benefits of helicopters and airplanes below:

	Helicopter	VS	Airplane
Description	A lot of helicopter pilots will describe a helicopter as an extension of your body. You can land and takeoff wherever you want as long as you have the right permissions. Broadly speaking, helicopters go slower than airplanes.		A lot of airplane pilots will talk about the freedom of travel that an airplane allows you. In an airplane, you can fly from point A to B as long as you can find a safe place to take off and land. Once you're in the air, broadly speaking, you will be able to go further and faster than a helicopter.
Training	Learning how to fly a helicopter is considered very difficult due to the hovering aspect of a helicopter. In order to get your license, you need to have at least 40 hours of training in a helicopter. However, most students need a little more time before going for the final exam, and on average use at least 70 to 90 hours.		Learning to fly an airplane is learning many different topics at once. In general, learning how to fly an airplane will be easier than a helicopter. In order to get your license, you need to have at least 40 hours of training in an airplane. However, most students need a little more time before going for the final exam, and on average use at least 60 to 80 hours.
Cost of training	Depends on what kind of helicopter, how many hours you'll need, your instructor, and your location. Training is generally more expensive than learning to fly an airplane.		Depends on what kind of airplane, how many hours you'll need, your instructor, and your location. Training is generally less expensive than learning to fly an helicopter.

Helicopter pilots and airplane pilots have a friendly rivalry about which aircraft is better. Sometimes it can feel like you're picking between two teams, so don't be surprised by a certain bias if you talk to either kind of pilot on which side you should choose. A helicopter decided to fly over just as I wrote that exact sentence, thinking Team Helicopter sponsored that flight.

According to 2021 U.S. Civil Airmen Statistics, less than 2% of total pilots in the US are helicopter pilots {not including pilots trained in the military). Therefore there will be an emphasis on airplanes as you continue reading the next chapters. And you're right in your observations that most pilots interviewed in this book are airplane pilots. So to make the debate between the two fair, I've included an equal number of arguments from both sides as to why you should their side:

Team Helicopter **VS** **Team Airplane**

Helicopters can land anywhere which makes for an "easy" rescue, they can hoist rescuers down and provide medical attention. Airplanes will only fly over. Planes also need runways. ... need I say more?

- Miles Weidman,
Aerial Fighter Pilot

There is no doubt that helicopters possess incredible abilities, and their usefulness and advantages are unparalleled in the aviation industry. They sadly carry an unwarranted reputation of being dangerous, largely due to lopsided media coverage, when in fact helicopters are arguably safer than planes in many respects due to their ability to land in small spaces even without an engine. Before you pass judgment on these amazing machines, be open-minded to the surprisingly graceful experience of helicopter flight!

- Jessica Meiris,
CFII helicopter pilot

I've always loved airplanes, how high they fly, how far they can go. You don't get that with helicopters. I used to dream of how it must feel to be free and certainly felt that feeling many times, during my around the world flight.

- Travis Ludlow,
World Record Pilot: Youngest Pilot to Fly Around the World

My fluids professor for engineering once told me, "Airplanes, even after they lose their engine, gracefully glide back to the ground, but helicopters, they get along by beating the air around them into submission." I love them both, but airplanes will always have my heart!

- Collin Craytor,
Flight Instructor,
Oklahoma University

Unfortunately (or luckily), you don't start out flying the super-fast fighter jets when you first start flying. In my world, it translates to driving an older vehicle before you save up the money to buy a nicer car when you've had your license for a while. Except in this case you don't just need to buy the nicer vehicle, you'll have to get additional approvals. This brings us to what kind of permissions and documents you'll need to fly. Throughout the book, you'll naturally notice a greater presence of airplanes, and of course, they are different in terms of operation, but most of the knowledge is transferable to helicopters.

Roll up your sleeves, it's about to get a little complicated. Broadly speaking in the U.S., there are six types of licenses issued by the FAA. Technically, these are not called licenses but called certificates. There are also other types of licenses, which are called ratings. Once you start looking up flight schools you'll start seeing these two words, certificates and ratings, a lot. Of all the pilots I spoke to, not very many were able to simply explain the difference between certificate and rating. Keep that in mind if you find yourself confused in a certificate and rating conversation in the future.

So what's the difference between certificate and rating? A certificate or a license is your permission to fly. The six types of certificates, listed in order of difficulty, are sports, recreational, private, commercial, instructor, and airline. You can start at the first one and move your way up, and the highest level you get supersedes the others. For example, if you get a private pilot's license, you can fly an airplane regulated for those with a sports license, but not the other way around. Each license has different requirements and allows for different permissions.

A rating is not what I originally thought it was. To me, it sounded like a measure of how well you fly. I was a little intimidated to learn that once you got your license, you would be rated by the FAA on your flight performance. I envisioned a rating system of pilots. I was wrong. Instead, a rating is a term used to indicate what type of aircraft you can fly. There are numerous types of ratings, including the permission to fly using instruments in the cockpit (instrument rating). Of if you want to fly a seaplane, this would also require an additional rating (seaplane rating).

And after an airplane exceeds a certain size, one also has to get a type rating for each kind of airplane one flies. In the U.S., that means that pilots can fly without a model-specific type rating for an aircraft with only one engine under a certain maximum weight. Typically this maximum weight is 5,700 kg or 12,500 lb. To put that in perspective if you want to transport a giraffe you'll need a type rating for the aircraft you're using for that flight. Each rating requires additional training.

If you find it confusing, remember that many I spoke with, who have hundreds and thousands of flight hours, still had a hard time explaining the difference between certificates and ratings. Though it is technically a certificate that you receive and not a license, I will continue to use the word license in this book. A goal of mine throughout this process is for you to build confidence in your learning by using layman's terms and no jargon.

So what license should you get first? Though the sports license and recreational license require less training than the private pilot license, those two also come with more restrictions. The most common starting point is therefore the private pilot license.This is the path that I am on.

The private pilot license allows you to transport passengers without another pilot in the cockpit. Yes, you're a pilot, but there are certain limitations. For instance what kind of weather you can fly in. The private pilot license only allows you to fly using only your eyes to see outside the cockpit. This means you can't take advantage of the instruments available in the cockpit. In order to fly in cloudy weather or worse, you will need to learn how to fly using instruments. Though one learns some basic instruments in private pilot training, the next natural step for most pilots is to pursue the instrument rating.

Finding the right education pathway

You've decided you want to get up in the clouds, but where do you start? No journey is the same, but traditionally the three main ways of becoming a pilot are local airports, full-time programs, and the military.

If you wanted to get started tomorrow, the easiest option would be to find a flight school at your local airport. Flight schools at your local airport are usually privately owned small businesses. Depending on the size of their business, the school might employ a few different instructors or it might be run and operated solely by the owner.

LOCAL AIRPORTS

In most cases, you'll be on an individual path to getting your license. The school will work with you directly to structure your journey. In the U.S., your training will follow a structure that the school has designed, which should result in covering all the requirements set by the Federal Aviation Association (FAA) for the private pilot license.

Good or bad, you set your own schedule. Meaning if work or life comes in the way, you can opt out of training and get back into it when you desire. You want to make sure you do research both on the school, the instructor and the fleet of helicopters and planes the school uses (more on this later). If you want to fly recreationally, this is your best option.

Most local airport schools are what's called Part 61. What does this mean? Part 61 allows the instructor to create a flexible time schedule and can adjust the training to your needs. The structure is made by the instructor or the school, there is no official standard curriculum required by law. He or she will prepare you for your final pilot exam, called the check ride. When you go to a Part 61 school your check ride will always be done with an official FAA representative. Other schools, mostly pilot programs at colleges, are Part 141. The major difference between Part 61 and 141 is the flexibility in curriculum and time schedule. For Part 61 there is greater flexibility, while Part 141 is set.

When discussing local flight schools you'll often hear the term FBO. FBO is not an abbreviation for a sister organization of the FBI, but rather a shorthand for fixed-base operator. Any company that has the right to do business at an airport is called FBO. In other words, they have the right approvals to offer you their services from the airport. Other services include refueling, maintenance, hangaring, and aircraft rentals.

The local flight school pathway can be compared to signing up to a local gym and hiring a personal trainer to lead you to your personal fitness goals. Sometimes students will forget that to become a good pilot they should put in the time and effort outside the time spent in class. Just like diet and exercise outside your time with a personal trainer will make the difference between an average and awesome performance.

It might be hard to remember in the overwhelm of learning this new skill, but at your local flight school, you are 100% in charge of your education. If you don't like an instructor, you can get a new one. If you don't want to study outside the cockpit, you don't technically have to (though you probably should). If you have a strange feeling about the state of the airplane, you don't have to fly it. If you get a promotion at work and don't have the time to commit, you can make that call. Good or bad you are the master of your own pilot training.

FULL-TIME TRAINING PROGRAMS

If you already know you want to be an airline pilot, the best course of action is probably to join a full-time training program. If you don't have a college degree, one option is to get a college degree from an accredited college or university that offers flight training. There are many programs around the country that offer aspiring pilots the required flight training alongside an academic degree. This is why joining one of these full-time alternatives can be both cost-efficient and a way to fast-track your training.

These colleges and full-time pilot programs are usually Part 141. You might remember that the Part 141 schools follow a stricter curriculum and time schedule. Another major perk of studying at a Part 141 school, is that instead of having to obtain the required 1,500 hours in order to get your airline transport pilot license (ATP), you'll only need 1000 hours. Part 141 in simple terms (and probably way too simplified for officials reading this book) means it follows a standardized curriculum made by the FAA and the students do so much studying flying and aviation that they get to put in fewer hours. How long does it take to rack up 1,500 hours you might wonder? In a good year, you'll probably be able to log 500 hours. Realistically it takes most people a few years to fulfill this requirement.

Founded originally in 1926, Embry-Riddle is the oldest and largest aeronautical university in the U.S. It is probably also the most well-known aviation school in the world and is often referred to as the Harvard Business School of the skies. The school offers a four-year program, the Aeronautical Science Degree, which teaches you the ins and outs of aviation while allowing you to take flight lessons three times a week. Other well-known aviation schools are the University of North Dakota, Purdue University, Liberty University, Lewis University, and Ohio State University.

An additional benefit of going to a college beyond a solid education in flying is exposure to the aviation industry. Depending on what college you go to, you get the perks of building connections with peers and professors, as well as being able to leverage a strong alumni network.

If you already have a college degree and know that you want to become an airline pilot, you might want to consider a fast-track flight school. These schools offer zero-to-hero classes where you can get all required flight training and licenses you would get at a four-year college program in less than a year. Some of these students join the school after finishing college, while others go through the program without a degree. There are also flexible programs that allow for students to work or study alongside the flying lessons, but these programs typically last longer.

One of the most common fast track schools is called ATP Flight School. In my conversation with a former student, David Gibbons, who entered the school after a career outside aviation, he said one of his favorite parts is the fast track to seniority in the airlines. At the airlines, the sooner you can get your seniority number, the sooner you get to climb up the ladder and get more flexibility. "This option is accessible to everyone, regardless of socio-economic status, gender, or background. ATP Flight School offers loans and an efficient way to becoming an airline pilot," he told me over the phone "It is accessible to everyone, but it's not attainable for everyone." He admitted that he had to sacrifice a lot in those years. His life was one-track-minded on flying, which did result in no social life. On the flip side, he experienced a strong community in the alumni of his school both during his training and after graduating.

As of early 2022, Delta Airlines dropped the requirement for a college degree to apply for open positions. In a press release the recruiting team stated "After a comprehensive review of our pilot hiring requirements, Delta has decided to make a four-year college degree 'preferred' rather than required for first officer candidates, effective immediately." The effect of this change from one of the major airlines is still playing out.

If you're not sure if you want to become an airline pilot, a fast-track program or even a pilot degree at a college might not be the best option. If you realize during your four years getting a pilot degree that you don't really enjoy flying, you still won't be able to complete your degree without graduating from flight training. A possibly better option for you if you think you might enjoy flying would be to look for a college that allows you to get a minor in flying. This will allow you to get flight training while you get a degree. That way you can start flying, but you're not on the hook to finish in order to graduate college.

Think it might be too late to change your career? Think again. Arizona-based Rachel Santana was inspired to become a pilot at her job. Not long after she started working at Southwest Airlines as a flight attendant, she set her eyes on the cockpit. She was encouraged by the pilots to pursue a pilot license. Her introduction flight was a gift from one of the pilots she worked with. After taking lessons less frequently than she wanted to, she enrolled to get a college degree at the University of North Dakota. Today she is a flight instructor in Arizona and on her way to becoming an airline pilot.

MILITARY

The last pathway to becoming a pilot is the military route. The specific requirements to qualify and what the training looks like differ widely depending on what country and what branch you join.In the U.S., you can enlist to become a pilot in the Air Force, Army, Coast Guard, Marine Corps, and the

Navy (as well as the two smaller branches Army National Guard and Air National Guard). Each of these branches also has different programs depending on if you join as a full-time active military member or a supporting part-time member in the Reserves. Broadly speaking most military pilot training programs require that you are an officer in order to apply. In most cases in order to become an officer you have to have a college degree and complete officer school. In the United States, one way of fulfilling this requirement is enrolling in one of the prestigious military academies, such as the Air Force Academy in Colorado. The Academy might have a low acceptance rate, but know that there are many ways to Rome. There are more than 1,500 American colleges that offer Reserve Officers' Training Corps (ROTC), which is an alternative to the military academies and prepares you to become an officer while in college.

The officer requirement has been around since the early days of aviation. Already in 1914, U.S. Army Captain Paul Warden Beck wrote in a statement about the importance of military pilots being officers There was simply too much additional responsibility beyond being a great pilot. He mentions that the ideal military pilot has an additional military skillset outside the cockpit, such as photography, reconnaissance, and the military significance of what he sees from the air. He wrote, "For all of these reasons we have concluded that we must rely on commissioned officers of the regular army or organized militia, trained in time of peace to fulfill their functions in time of war." Beck was the first pilot to be awarded the "Military Aviator" badge and spent much of his career lobbying for a structure you still see in the backbone in the flight schools across the branches today.

Once you're admitted to pilot school, many of the branches today have a pre-flight school screening which is taught by civilians in similar airplanes that you'll see at your local airport flight schools. The screening is almost like dating before marriage. 25 or so hours in the cockpit is usually enough time to identify if someone isn't physically or mentally fit for the pilot program or in many cases the candidate realizes they aren't ready or interested in committing to flying. Candidates who don't proceed in the pilot training program are placed in other roles for the remaining years of their military contract. You might not be committing to pilot school, but you are now potentially blind dating other commitments in the military. If you get to graduate pilot training, you're definitely married to flying. From that point on you will spend the next months and potentially years living and breathing flying.

After the pre-flight school screening, there are usually two phases, primary and advanced pilot training. The primary phase starts on the ground with a heavy focus on theory, including topics such as navigation, aerodynamics, and weather. After finishing theoretical classes, also referred to as ground school, you finally get to start training in an actual airplane again. What that airplane is and for how long varies according to which military branch you end up at. During this phase, one can fill out written forms to get the FAA to issue a private pilot license, and depending on the hours and training completed, further licenses and ratings. One retired military pilot I spoke to missed this opportunity and has regretted it ever since. "All my days were already filled with flying, so I didn't feel like being bothered doing the small additional work, now I wish I had".

During the advanced stage, the students get practical knowledge and the ones who graduate get their wings and get assigned an aircraft, or what the military often refers to as an airframe. During this time you're always evaluated and graded while learning an insane amount of new information. Many explained it as "drinking from a fire hose" while trying to survive. A military pilot told me "One morning you can feel like a rockstar, but be kicked out of the program at the end of that same day."

You're graded on attitude, mental and physical ability. These grades are essential at the end of flight school because the top students are first in line when choosing what kind of aircraft and location you're off to next. Of course, the needs of the military are taken into account, but the better you've done the more likely you're going to get your top pick. "There are of course some that wash out and don't qualify to become pilots. But in most cases, if you show that you are always studying, trying hard to learn, and really want this, they will do everything to help you succeed" an officer from the U.S. Air Force told me.

The intensity of military training was echoed by military pilots from other countries as well. Jan Slangen, the former Italian Aerobatic Team pilot, told me he had to fight hard to stay in his class. Only half of the 100 pilots who started were allowed to continue, and of those, only a handful, were able to complete the whole program. "You have to put more effort in", he explains.

The four main types of airframes one can be assigned in the military are fighter jets (think Tom Cruise in Top Gun), Ospreys (looks like if an airplane and a helicopter had a baby), helicopters (self-explanatory indeed, but usually a lot larger than the ones you see your local police or news station fly) or multi-engine airplanes (there are a lot of planes that fit into this category from radar planes to giant transportation planes that make you question how large the world actually is).

Who will you meet in military flight school? All kinds of people who wanted to get up in the skies. Some of the military pilots I spoke to had known all their lives they wanted to become aviators, others randomly walked into it.

Mike Van Wyk, a former U.S. Navy Blue Angels pilot, has a picture of himself in front of the famous Blue Angels Fat Albert from an airshow he went to in second grade. His dream lay dormant while he pursued a degree in music in college, before later joining officer training. The first time he was actually in an airplane was on the way to the military. Albert Perez, retired U.S. Marine Corp helicopter pilot shared that experience "I had never been on an airplane before I was heading to the military." Originally scared of flying, little did he know that his career would entail hundreds and hundreds of hours in the skies.

As a part of my research, I was fortunate to be able to stand on the Naval Air Station Point Mugu runway and witness pilots practicing landings. Hour after hour the pilots would do "touch and go's" and every single time one person would take notes and grade every performance. These were not new pilots, but seasoned pilots who were training to become better. I got dizzy watching them and I wasn't even in the cockpit.

Most likely you will not find this quality of training when going to the local airport or flight college, and you most definitely will not get it for free and on a paid salary. If your long-term goal is to become an airline pilot, you'll only be required 750 hours to get your airline transport pilot license instead of the 1,500 that you need if you get your license at the local airport. However, these benefits come with a large personal sacrifice that comes automatically by signing up to be a part of military defense.

Unlike the civilian paths, you cannot just quit one day. You are under legal obligation with the military. If you join the US military, you'll be serving at least ten years. If you join the Royal Air Force in the UK, you're signing up for 12 years of minimum service. And every few years you will be asked to rejoin the military and if you decide to continue it usually means a new assignment in a different location.

These three paths are different in the level of commitment and resources required. For your local airport experience, you'll be in charge of your learning experience (if you don't like your instructor, you can change), while in college and the military you will have a more controlled path (if you don't like your instructor, you can't change as easily).

The paths to becoming a pilot are not always followed as black and white. You will find that many pilots have mixed experience from two or even all three. Jaden Risner fell in love with flying early as he spent a lot of time in the air as an accompanied minor flying between his mom and dad who lived in different cities. He grew up by Santa Monica airport and spent most of his youth at air shows at the Museum of Flying. He started studying aviation as a young teen and soloed when he was 16 before he could even drive by himself. He flew recreationally before heading to the U.S. Navy where he earned his wings of gold in 2009 and has been flying for the military since. He ended up going with helicopters in the Navy and has maintained his airplane private license in the civilian world.

Carl Valeri loved building model airplanes growing up, but didn't think he would ever be able to fly one. One day in college the person next to him said "you know you can fly those right?" Valeri soon started taking flying lessons but didn't approach it professionally. Dedicated to putting the degree in computers that his parents so generously had paid for, he built a successful software company. But then one day, Valeri decided it was time to get paid doing the thing he loved most and decided it was time to join a full-time flight school. Today Valeri is not only a Jet Blue pilot, but also runs the Aviation Careers podcast and helps others chase their aviation dreams.

Bruce Rose is one who took his recreational flying to the

next level. He started flying at 17 years old but decided early on that a professional flying career wasn't for him. That didn't stop him from going after the most advanced licenses and ratings. Today he has an airline transport pilot license with many type ratings, including for Falcon 900 and Global Express. He enjoys flying all over the world with his family in his spare time. All of this while being the CEO and founder of the Carrington Companies, one of the largest real estate service companies in the U.S.

Phil McConkey was told by many that he was crazy thinking he could achieve his dream of becoming a professional football player after many years in the U.S. Navy as a helicopter pilot. Boy, did McConkey prove them wrong? Not only did he become a professional player playing for several teams, including Green Bay Packers and San Diego Chargers, but he also went on the win the Superbowl in 1986 with the New York Giants. And if anyone is a good example of making your own path despite what others might say or despite non-ideal timing, it is McConkey. He started in the military a few years after the Vietnam world when public opinion was generally not in the favor of the military. Then he went on to start his professional football career at 27, a lot later than the norm. And when the rest of the world was worried about a global financial crisis in 2009, he launched his own financial firm, Academy Securities. Now in his 60s, Phil McConkey says, "I am just getting started". No one can predict the future, but we got to start somewhere. The next step is finding the right school.

Finding the right school

If you have settled on either the local airport track or a full-time program, you'll need to identify the right school. For the sake of national security, you won't have this kind of flexibility to decide if you go the military route. If that's the route you want to go, this section might not be applicable to you, but will still help you prepare for the journey ahead with helpful information.

If flying your family around on adventures is a bucket list item for you, but you don't intend to do it professionally, a local flight school is probably the best option. If you're set on a pilot career and have ruled out the military route, a college degree or accelerated flight school program is your best bet. A local flight school is still an option, but some will argue it takes more time and effort than structured full-time programs. You'll have to decide which works best for you.

Regardless of your chosen track, you should write a list of items that would make the experience best for you. Here is a section from my personal checklist:

- not more than 30 minutes of driving from my house
- offers options to change instructors should I want to mix it up
- have a flexible schedule so I can book my lessons around my ever-changing schedule
- have additional social community activities attached to it
- have been around for at least 3 years

I know it's hard to make a list of an experience you're not familiar with, but it's good to have a personal standard before looking around. Kind of like how single people have been told by well-meaning-already-settled friends for decades to make a list of must-haves and deal-breakers in their ideal perfect relationship. You can't know how anything in life will pan out, but it's good to have reflected before being overwhelmed with marketing material. Your list will probably expand as you learn more. Do know when you sit down and look for flight schools, expect to see a lot of 90s design websites and outdated links. Fortunately, we're not judging marketing materials, we're looking for the right school for your goals.

After you've finalized your ideal pilot experience list here are some key things to look for when deciding on a school:

- The kind of planes or helicopters you will be training in. On this point, if you see something strange, say something. You would if you were renting a car! You might not know as much about airplanes as you do about cars at this point, but always investigate!
- Ask them about their maintenance schedule. If the school has its own maintenance department even better!
- Make sure to estimate the distance to your house. A lesson will usually last two hours, so keep that in mind for your overall lesson planning.
- Cost. If it seems too cheap, it probably is! More on this later.
- Financing options. Some local airport schools offer discounts if you schedule many lessons in advance. If you're going to college, there might scholarships and financial aid available. More on this topic in a later chapter.
- Ask to see their syllabus. Not all schools will have one but every school should have a general sense of what they are teaching and in what order. If they don't, this might be a red flag.
- If you're looking to make a career in aviation, you will want to know what additional resources the school provides. Examples include brand recognition in the industry, a good relationship with the aviation business, and a strong alumni network.
- Even if you're not approaching flying as a career, you might want a community of pilots. Ask the school if they host events for the students and alumni to meet.

- Ask the school for prior student testimonials. When making a decision I like to do plenty of research and hear from both sides of the spectrum.

Finding the right instructor

Starting flying lessons can be overwhelming. There is a lot of new information thrown at you from the very first visit to a flight school. It's like stepping into a new world with its own rules and a brand new language. You may not want to stop and ask too many unnecessary questions because it's humbling to be the new kid on the block. You want to get situated in this new world quickly. You want to blend in as soon as possible. Many student pilots have quit flying because they rushed into the process and chose the wrong instructor. But by spending some extra time up front to ensure you choose the right instructor, this can be avoided.

When you identify your ideal school, you might also find the right instructor in the process. But if not, don't be afraid to spend some additional time on this. If you're training in the military or attending flight school, you most likely will be assigned your instructors. It might still be beneficial for you to reflect on what kind of instructor and teaching styles you prefer.

Create a list of what attributes you are looking for in a flight instructor. You should consider how you best learn new information and what that environment looks like. Do you prefer taking your time? Or maybe you prefer your lessons to be purely technical and absolutely no small talk? Are you a visual learner? Auditory? Prefer reading? Get it all down on a piece of paper. When you have made your list, you can ask the school you have identified if that sounds like one of their instructors.

"You'll want to find an instructor you'll want to eat lunch with after class," a corporate pilot who wanted to remain anonymous told me. He compared it to dating. It's better to spend some extra time getting to know the person rather than settling. "You want to find an instructor that you can be friends with, but also that can keep you accountable. Short of dating, the relationship with your flight instructor will be your most expensive relationship." You decide what is best for you, but know that you'll be spending many hours in the cockpit with this person.

An instructor can make a huge difference in a pilot's progression and overall experience. According to Italian pilot, Massimo Tammaro, a good instructor is fundamental. Just like in the workplace where bosses can have a big impact on someone's career. However, Tammaro doesn't necessarily believe a tough instructor is a bad thing. "Having a tough instructor is ok as long as they are clever. As long as you can learn, it will outweigh an instructor's toughness," he believes. YouTuber and fighter jet pilot Pierre-Henri "ATÉ" Chuet felt that he had learned more from bad instructors than the good ones. In his experience, bad instructors showed him a good example of how he did not want to be and he used it as motivation to be a better pilot and eventually flight instructor.

Many will be surprised at first to learn that many flight instructors are comparatively new to flying themselves. It is a common route for aspiring airline pilots to become certified as flight instructors to get paid while building the 1,500 hours needed to advance to the airlines. In order to get your certified flight instructor license (CFI), you must have a commercial license with an instrument rating and have logged 250 hours. Though it's not an official airline requirement, airlines also like seeing a CFI on a candidate's resume.

Some would argue that this system attracts a lot of pilots

who lack the motivation and skills to be great instructors. Others will argue that teaching is the best way to truly learn to fly. Many student pilots have experienced that their instructor quit teaching rather abruptly when he or she had flown the hours they needed to move on in their pilot career. Keep in mind, even though these instructors might be new to teaching, some of them are highly motivated and excellent teachers. Everyone has to start somewhere. There are always going to be great teachers who are new and bad teachers who are experienced and vice versa.

A great instructor is an instructor that matches what YOU are looking for and what works best for you. Make sure to spend some time getting to know any potential flight instructor. Everyone who knows me, knows I love asking (maybe too many) questions to truly understand new concepts. Yes, at times I am that annoying classmate who will ask in detail until I understand. By asking many questions in a first conversation I can tell if an instructor would get impatient. And if you find yourself having a hard time following what he or she is saying or just in general feel like you are not jiving, it might be a sign. But if you're unsure, you can always ask for another conversation. Though you'll find a checklist of questions to ask your potential instructors below, know that this list cannot replace your own instincts.

Sometimes the instructor can also sense a bad fit. "I am often able to tell within the first few lessons if I'm the right instructor for a student. If I'm not, I will talk to my colleagues and suggest a better fit based on what I know of that student's learning style" says Pauline Hulbert, an airline pilot and flight instructor from South Africa. A good instructor will not take offense if you want a different instructor, because they will want to see you succeed and do everything to support you in that journey.

You might have to spend some additional time looking for your instructor or you might find them right away. And you might find that it's not just one instructor, but multiple. Flying with different instructors will give you a broader knowledge base. And you are guaranteed to pick up tips and tricks from different instructors. Miles O'Brien, a long-time pilot based in Florida, spoke passionately about this: "Having many instructors will make you a better pilot. You will learn different techniques and perspectives from different instructors."

When you start looking for flight instructors, you might not be sure what to ask. Here are some questions for interviewing a potential instructor:

What are your short and long-term pilot career goals? If your instructor plans to build hours and doesn't really enjoy teaching, this question can help identify that. If your instructor fits the bill but plans to leave for the airlines in the short term future, you'll be less surprised when it happens knowing it ahead of time. It's an obvious plus if the instructor loves to teach and wants to continue doing so. But also be aware that there has been a tradition for some instructors to lose interest in growing as pilots. Some of the more seasoned instructors might be set in their ways and just looking to make their paycheck. You want to find a happy medium between experience and interest in teaching. Too much of just one is probably not going to be the best instructor.

What excites you about being a flight instructor? This question identifies if the instructor has passion and interest in teaching. We all have bad days from time to time, but you're paying for someone to pay attention to the details of your training and, above all, your safety. No need to say, but if the instructor shows no interest in flying or teaching, he or she might not be able to keep you focused or interested in your learning plateaus.

How much will this cost me? When asking for a financial overview of what your training will cost, you should already know what to expect in terms of the price range in your local area. If you're presented with a price that is too high or too low, you should definitely inquire further why that is. If you're trying to set aside an allocated amount to flying, you might want to add some additional funds to take account of some extra lessons needed here and there. More on this in a later chapter.

How long will it take me? Keep in mind that most students will need more than the required 40 hours, in most cases between 60 to 80 hours, to pass the FAA final practical exam. Anyone who promises you'll be able to do it at the bare minimum should have a pretty good answer to why they can make that happen.

What kind of aircraft do you have experience with? It can be a plus to have an instructor with a wide experience. A pilot who has flown a few different aircraft will have a broader knowledge.

What is your teaching style? This question is designed to match your best learning style with your instructor's teaching style. If the potential instructor relies highly on reading assignments and you are a visual learner, you might run into problems.

What are your expectations of your students? Some instructors might be more demanding than others, or the other way around. If you're someone who likes to be driven to your maximum potential, you'll want to identify that in an instructor. Any instructor should expect a student at a bare minimum to prepare for class. If you have many other commitments that don't allow you to spend a ton of extra time studying outside of class, you'll want to work with your instructor to build this into your flight lessons. Studying is a crucial part of becoming a successful pilot, but there are ways to make it work for you with the right instructor.

How would you like to receive feedback from a student? If you sense any resistance to this question, I would personally run in the opposite direction. You need to be able to know that you can confidently give feedback to your instructor.

I want to achieve XYZ by December 10th, how can we make this happen? If you want to plan a trip to visit family or your goal is to join the airlines, tell your instructor. If the goal is achievable, the instructor should be able to create a clear plan for you. A good instructor will also tell you if your plan is too ambitious and unrealistic. The old customer service saying "underpromise, over deliver" goes a long way here.

May I speak to some of your former students? It's never a bad idea to ask your instructor for some testimonials. A good instructor will not take offense to this, and if they do there is your sign right there. An exception to asking this question is the brand new instructors that might not have had many students in the past. Even though newer instructors have less experience, you might discover that they put in extra effort to prove to you that they are really motivated.

If you find that you can't keep up with the instructor as he or she is answering the above question, that might be a sign that it might not be the right fit. In many cases, it's not you, it's them. One instructor might be a great fit for another student, and not for you and that's ok. Don't be afraid to stick to the ideal instructor checklist you made. In the words of American investor, Charlie Munger: "No wise pilot, no matter how great his talent and experience, fails to use his checklist."

Do I really have to go to one more school?
When you start researching schools you'll start seeing the term "ground school" used a lot. It might seem like it's an actual school, but it's actually a nickname for the theory classes. It is the stuff you learn on the ground while not in the cockpit, hence the term ground school. Nowadays you can enroll in ground schools online, some are even offered for free.

If you enroll in a local flight school, ground school is not required. Many instructors would still absolutely recommend you do it. The classes are meant to teach basic principles of flying, which can help you become a better and safer pilot. And if you study hard in ground school you can maximize your instructor time. If you join the military or full-time flight school be aware you'll be grounded. Not really, but you should expect to spend some time in the classroom before getting into the cockpit.

One benefit from attending ground school in person is that you might make friends with other aspiring pilots. I personally met one of my closest friends in theory class when I was getting my driver's license. The friendship maintains today.

In the end, only you will know the best pathway forward, including what type of aircraft, what kind of education, the right school, and the ideal instructor. We all have different aspirations in life and we all have different ways of learning.

As you continue reading through this book know that you can always close your eyes and chair-fly your ideal scenario. Or you might be inspired by someone's else story and envision yourself doing something similar. And don't forget to keep those checklists handy. It's easy to waiver when we are in unchartered territories and overwhelmed by new information, but these checklists can be key. Checklists can keep you grounded and remind you of your standards.

CHAPTER THREE
Aviate, Navigate, Communicate

TO START SOMETHING NEW CAN be terrifying. If it's not, is it really worth it? But you have to learn to walk before you run. In this chapter, we'll walk through some basic lingo of flying. Any trained pilot or flight instructor can provide a lot more details as to what flying is and what it isn't, but I intentionally kept this chapter at a bird's eye view (no pun intended). By knowing the basics before entering that cockpit, my hope is that you'll be better prepared than I was for my first lesson. By giving you the basic terminology, you might understand more of what's going on during that first flight.

Let's for a minute think of learning to fly as learning a new language. Most language classes start with your "hello", "how are you?", and the words you need to know to order a glass of wine, to get you acquainted with the language. Everyone knows that these phrases won't be of much help in deeper conversations. To have the vocabulary to discuss complex topics, such as the meaning of life, takes time. Time to build your understanding and develop your vocabulary. This is true for speaking pilot too. So don't expect to understand everything in your first lesson. Rather get into that cockpit and lean back, observe and enjoy the foreign landscape. And realize that the person you're sitting next to was also brand new at some point. And one day you might be bringing this brand new experience to someone else. And at that moment you can look back and giggle about how much you've learned since you started.

As British philosopher, Alain de Botton, once said "Anyone who isn't embarrassed by who they were last year probably isn't learning enough." It's since become one of my favorite quotes to live by. My hope for this chapter is to help give a perspective of the journey ahead from a high-level overview. And how others experienced the journey before you. Remember confidence is built with time as you learn to trust your abilities.

Aviate

THERE IS A SAYING YOU'LL hear often as you start flying: aviate, navigate, communicate. The saying is a reminder of what your priorities are when you're in the cockpit. You fly first, then you look around, and lastly, you speak your intentions. Putting it in more familiar terms, if you're driving a car in bad weather, you'll first focus on steering the car, before you look at the GPS, before calling anyone to tell them about what's going on. Aviate, navigate, communicate. The saying is said to have been introduced after the fatal Everglades accident in December 1972. That flight ended tragically because the pilots were focused on fixing what turned out to be a false alarm rather than flying the aircraft. Let's start diving into the first term "aviate": flying the plane.

In order to get your private license, aka your entry ticket to be able to fly around alone, you need 40 hours in the air. This requirement is the same whether you're learning to fly a helicopter or an airplane. Every pilot has a flying journal that records all the time she or he spends aloft. This journal is called the logbook. With technology, a lot of pilots have moved on to keeping these records digitally, but most pilots spoke still keep their leather-bound pages up to date. Anytime you're going to a flight lesson you want to make sure to bring yours so you can log your flying time.

Back to those required 40 hours. Just one average American

workweek you say? Hold on, cowboy, not so fast. You see those are the minimum hours, but that doesn't mean your instructor (or you if you're honest with yourself) will deem you ready for the final check ride. Learning fast does not equate to understanding. Besides you have to account for pre-flight time and debrief after each lesson, so many of your lessons you will not be able to log 60 minutes in your logbook.

During your 40 hours, you will need to fly with an instructor to get specific lessons for 20, and you'll need to fly 10 hours yourself. Here is how the FAA breaks it down:

20 hours with instructor:	10 hours solo (yup only you in the cockpit)
Must at minimum include: - 3 hours cross country flights (from airport to airport, no one is sending you abroad - yet) - 3 hours night flights (flying in the dark is a different ballgame) - 3 hours flying with instruments - 3 hours flight test prep	Must at minimum include: - 5 hours of solo cross country flight (including at least 150 nautical miles total distance with full stop landings at 3 points) - 10 takeoffs and 10 landings to a full stop at an airport

For each one of these requirements, your instructor will have to sign their name to say that you've completed these. In other words, you're most likely going to need some additional time on one or several items. Make sure to study outside of the cockpit, and you'll find that you'll learn concepts, if not always faster, but better.

Your first flight

Treat your first flight like a ride at Disneyland. It's only magical if you don't try to understand how it all works. Can you imagine how not magical your day at the happiest place on the planet would be if you were trying to figure out how it all really worked?

On a video call from Arizona, Greg Brown, recently inducted into Flight Instructor Hall of Fame at the National Business Aviation Association, recommended asking for a longer introductory flight if possible. "A full 2 hours experience allows you to get a little more comfortable in the cockpit, more than a 20-minute introductory flight" explains Brown. If necessary, call to schedule a first lesson instead of an introductory flight.

And to ensure that the first flight is magical, I made a pre-flight FIRST lesson checklist that you can better prepare for your first flying adventure:

- Wear clothing that you can move around easily. You don't want to worry about showing your behind while climbing into the cockpit. You also want to consider the weather. Being too hot can invite unwelcome air sickness. But at the same time, it's harder to think about flying if you're cold.
- Wear shoes you can easily move around in. That might mean dropping the heels, but also big work boots can be a little too much too.
- Bring a pair of sunglasses. My choice is always a cool pair of aviators.
- Eat a good meal.
- Be hydrated.
- Charge your phone. I often forget to take pictures, but I am grateful I have one from my intro flight.
- Plan ahead, as in go to bed early the night before and be on time.
- Realize before going there, you're not going to understand everything. Envision yourself going on a vacation to a foreign country, chances are you wouldn't have an unrealistic expectation of knowing the culture, language, and routes as soon as you arrived. You

wouldn't be embarrassed to ask for directions or a translation. Treat your flying lesson the same way. Don't be scared to ask questions. And more importantly, don't be hard on yourself for not understanding it all

- Bring a notebook
- Enjoy the flight!

So what will your first introductory flight look like? It will vary from location to location, and from instructor to instructor. Here are some observations made from a collective of pilots reflecting on their first lesson:

Unlike getting into a car, when you first show up at the airport, you have to do a pre-flight walkthrough of the airplane. At most schools, you'll be asked to be a part of this pre-flight checklist the very first time. You and your instructor will go around the aircraft and make sure everything is as it should be. You'll be under the wing checking the fuel level and on your toes (if you're short like me) checking the oil.

Once you've gone around the aircraft on the outside, you'll be in the cockpit with your instructor. Many have not prepared for how crammed that can feel. And once the engines are fired up, you'll quickly realize that helicopters and airplanes are loud. In order to communicate with your instructor, you'll be wearing headphones. This part can be very disorienting at first. You see you'll be hearing more than your instructor's voice on the headphones. We'll get back to those voices over the radio later in this chapter. Just know, that most pilots I spoke to were pretty intimidated at that point.

Another element that has confused many that first lesson, is if you're flying a plane, it's hard to see something right in front of your airplane. It's not you, it's the way that planes are designed. From then on you "drive" the plane, called taxiing, on the roads of the airport to another spot, where you complete another checklist. Depending on the instructor, he or she might do this by themselves or include you. Then you'll taxi towards the runway and take off. Once up in the air, most instructors will let you be at the controls while they teach you some basics of flying. Sometimes your instructor will be speaking in code with someone else and you'll think he or she is speaking to you. It's confusing and magical and overwhelming and exciting all at once.

Then after a while, it's time to go back to the ground, and the instructor takes the controls to facilitate the landing. And at this point, know that most pilots before you have had a major cognitive moment of dissonance. Cognitive dissonance in case you're unfamiliar is having two competing thoughts at once. In this case, for decades pilots have had two competing thoughts: "OMG this is the coolest thing I've ever experienced" and "How will I ever be able to do this on my own?" Hopefully, you have a great experience and decide to continue towards your license.

Phase 1

For the first part of your education, you'll be practicing the basics of flying. High level, this means rolling out to the runway, taking off, flying in the air, and landing. Of course, there is a lot that goes into being able to do that, but in summary, you're learning the basics of flying.

While most find that taxiing and takeoff are pretty straightforward, many students struggle with landings at first. "Landings was unnatural to me at first", says seasoned pilot Lee Abrams. He is not the only one that struggles with the counterintuitive of the landing. It is not uncommon for students to bounce on their first (or many) landings. But with time and practice, like everything else, your build the skills and the confidence. When you practice your landings, you'll land only to take off right away, which is why it's called touch and go.

As you can imagine building the confidence to taxi, take off, fly and land will take a few hours. But once you have done it over and over again enough times to show your instructor that you are capable to do this on your own (yes, solo!), one day she or he will jump out that side door and let you take off on your own. Traditionally your instructor won't let you know until that moment happens so you don't have built-up nerves the day before. How many hours will it take before you're ready for your first solo? It strictly varies from case to case. Most students will take an average of 15 hours to get to the point where they can go up in the air on their own.

First solo

I wish the energy that came across when I asked pilots to recount their first solo could be bottled. Jamie Beckett is a Florida-based flight instructor who's had the chance to see many students solo during his career. "It is incredible to see someone come out of the cockpit after their first solo. You can see it in their eyes that they're thinking "If I can fly an airplane, I can do a lot more than I thought in this life!"", he says. And a lot of pilots shared stories of that moment.

Though it was many years ago for retired U.S. Air Force pilot Rob Balzano, still remembers his first solo in a glider. A glider is towed behind an airplane before it's released into the air. "The airplane dropped the glider and it got very, very quiet. The feeling of successfully landing for the first time has been hard to beat ever since." And Balzano flies fighter jets for a living.

For many of the pilots, I interviewed it was so many years ago that it was hard to remember the details of that first solo. But entrepreneur and founder of Hawke Media, Erik

Huberman, solo'ed around the time I was writing this book. "First solo I wasn't sure that I actually knew how to land! It was irrational because I had done it a ton. But there was something about the first time I landed, that I then felt I could really do it. Once I did that, then it was easy."

So what will your first solo look like? The first time you solo you land and go right back up and repeat usually three to four times. This is called touch and go, and you'll get used to this practice of repetition right after an accomplishment. Repeating something difficult right after you've done it once and doing it successfully multiple times in a row will help build confidence. It's a practice I've adopted in my life because it's genius.

My friends aren't too excited that I've adopted this practice in my daily life, just ask one of my dearest friends who was struggling to understand one of those way-too-complicated-not-sure-how-they-manage-to-sell-so-many-wrap-around-your-baby-blankets. She was struggling (for super obvious reasons, those things are more complicated than a Rubik's cube), but when she figured it out the first time, I made her do it over and over again.

Worried you'll never be fully ready to solo? Not one single person could with confidence say that they weren't a little nervous and had a little doubt about being ready. Including U.S. national aerobatic champion and legendary aviator, Patty Wagstaff. Reflecting on her first solo, she told me "I couldn't believe "they" let me do it." Other pilots shared the sentiment that the absence of an instructor made the cockpit feel a lot larger. One pilot said, "As soon as my instructor stepped out, I remember thinking the airplane was way too big for me to fly."

So maybe you won't feel ready, but once your instructor tells you that it's your time to solo, you'll have to trust that they know you are. There are hundreds of YouTube videos of people who show up to their lesson one day and are surprised by the instructor that this is the day for their first solo. It's always inspiring to see someone smile as they complete their solo landing. And seeing people from all corners of the world, different genders and ages, hopefully, will instill what this book is all about. That you too, can one day solo your own aircraft.

Phase 2

You've soloed. Now what? Until now you've been practicing flying around the area of one airport. Now it is time to welcome your instructor back into the cockpit. During this phase, you'll learn how to fly at night, a little bit about flying with instruments, and how to plan for a flight.

Learning to fly at night is something that many pilots find challenging. Navigating from the air during the day can be hard enough, but at night it's even harder to spot an airport from other lit up buildings. That being said a long-time military pilot told me that flying at night will always be more challenging, no matter what stage you're at. "Flying at night is tough, especially as you grow older. Your senses are naturally dulled." So take your time and do the best you can, and you'll have a safe and fun night flight. Most pilots who are serious about flying will eventually move on to get additional training which makes flying at night time even safer.

During this stage, you will also have at least three lessons where you learn to use some basic instruments. At this point, you are given the knowledge of how to use them, but not rely on them. The flight preparation lessons will teach you how to read the weather and plan your trips so that you can do that with confidence.

When you're becoming a private pilot, you will be learning how to fly using what is called Visual Flight Rules. It should come as no surprise at this point that no one calls it Visual Flight Rules, but rather use the abbreviation, VFR. Flying VFR means you'll be using your eyes to look outside the cockpit to navigate. This also means that when weather blocks your view, think clouds, rain, and fog, you won't be allowed to fly with your private pilot license unless you can safely fly around them.

In your training for your license, you'll get a taste of what it's like to fly using only aids for navigation. To make sure you can't see out the window, your instructor will give you a long cap visor (think casino dealers) or fogged-out glasses with a small area at the bottom that's clear. This, my friend, is nicknamed flying under the hood. It's the taste of what flying with instruments inside clouds is like. But you won't be able to rely on navigating with instruments, Instrument Flight Rules, referred to as IFR, until after you've finished your private pilot license and gotten additional training in instruments. This additional training and test are called Instrument Rating, once you've completed that stage it will be possible for you to say "I am a private pilot with an instrument rating."

This stage is meant to hone your flying skill and to prepare you for your own solo country hours. You have taken the aircraft for many spins around the airport, but you've always parked her in the same spot. Now it's time to go further. It's time for your cross-country lessons. You should at this point have flexed your flying muscles quite a lot. And in the process built the confidence you need to take off from grounds that have now become very familiar to you, your local airport, to uncharted terrority, another close-by airport. When your instructor believes you're up for it, you go on your first solo cross-country flight.

Phase 3

Your first solo cross-country flight is similar to your first solo in nerves for most pilots. At this point not only are you flying on your own, but you are going places! Ahead of this flight, you've made the flight plan and you're going on your very first road trip. Many times instructors will make you get a signature from someone or have you call them as proof that you made it.

Grace McKellar won't forget her first cross-country flight. Based in the UK, she had to fly across to three different airports. Already warmer than usual from nerves, it turned out to be warmer than usual on this summer day. It didn't help that she thought she had gotten lost at some point. Regardless of her few moments of thoughts, McKellar aced her first cross-country trip. And she told me of an incredible feeling of accomplishment. Another pilot I spoke with specifically asked that I remind every aspiring pilot to remember to use the bathroom before their cross-country and to bring a bottle of water and some snacks!

Keep in mind that the order of lessons might be different from the order I listed above at the school you find. The key part is that you complete all the requirements.

Final check ride

And one day it's eventually time for your final exam. You've studied hard for this moment and you'll do a check ride with an FAA representative. Much like any other exam you've taken in your life, they can ask you anything from the required curriculum. Your experience will greatly vary based on who that person is. Some are very strict, others are rather laidback. It is extremely common to be nervous about this exam, but you have to trust that you have the skills it requires to show that you are soon to become a private pilot.

And here is a thing about this test you, of course, want to

pass. Like other exams outside of the pilot world, life will go on if you fail. One pilot I spoke to, who will remain unnamed, failed his first check ride. With some hindsight perspective, he realized he wasn't as prepared as he needed to be and after some additional training he was able to get back into the cockpit and get that license.

On the day of your final check ride, you'll be wearing a t-shirt you're not worried about. Tradition has it that your flight instructor will cut off the back part. Legends say this tradition started because back in the old days the instructor would sit behind the student and pull their shirt to yell their feedback in lieu of the non-existent radios. Cutting the back of that shirt was a symbolic celebration that the student no longer needed the instructor's guidance. In other cultures, such as Britain, the celebration entails the instructor soaking their student in water. If you want a combination, you can always ask, right?

If you continue your pilot journey, most likely this will not be your last check ride. And most pilots I spoke to admitted to still getting nervous about check rides. They even have a term for it, "checkoritus". If you decide on a career with the airlines, know that you'll be forced to do check rides every 9 months to demonstrate recurrence. Jim Baird, a retired United Airlines captain with over 45 years of experience explained: "Every check ride is a challenge. Check rides are stressful by design". Even if you pass or fail on your first check ride, you'll soon be holding your very own private pilot license. And with that license comes a new title and a new world: you're a pilot and will be warmly welcomed into the exclusive ranks of pilots!

Navigate

FIRST, YOU AVIATE, NOW IT'S time to navigate: There are actually two types of navigation in flying: navigation on earth and navigation in the air. It's easy to forget that you have to navigate the earth in order to get into the air. Until teleportation is a thing, you'll need to learn how to get to the takeoff area.

Airports are like small little towns with their own parking spots, freeways, and exits. Just like in your local area, some places you need special permission or organizational belonging to enter, some are free for all. Every airport has its own map that shows the runways, the parking spots, and the pathways in between. Like moving to a new city and learning the names of new streets can be a little disorienting, the airport can be a little confusing at first. Roads are often given one-letter names, such as A, B, and C. While runways are given a number accompanied with either R or L, indicating if it's right or left. The airport maps, called airport diagrams, are overwhelming at first sight. But luckily, like moving to a new city, with time you'll start getting familiar.

Your starting point is the aircraft's parking spot, often called an apron or a ramp. From there you have to use the airport roads to navigate to the runway. Depending on the size of your airport, there might be a few stops along the way. If you're flying a helicopter, you can't roll anywhere since there are no wheels, but you'll have assigned areas you hover in between. Regardless of what kind of aircraft you end up in, moving around the airport is called taxiing.

Unlike roads for cars, where the yellow line indicates the separation of traffic, at the airport, you'll want to line up the airplane to follow the yellow line. There is a reason for that you see. If you're on the yellow line the wings are perfectly aligned.

When you get to your takeoff area, you'll need to navigate in what direction you're going immediately after you have taken off. After you've completed, this your journey begins. If you're practicing landings you'll most likely stay in what is called the traffic pattern. The traffic pattern of the airport is the lineup for who gets to land. In other words, it's like a circle of cool kids in airplanes waiting for their turn in line. When you are going further on your cross-country trips, you'll go outside of the traffic pattern and fly towards whatever your destination is. When you reach your destination you will line up in that airport's traffic pattern and once again wait for your turn to land.

Navigating in the air is similar to navigating down on earth, though naturally more advanced. Despite the freedom, flying gives you, getting from point a to point b requires a little bit more planning. There are two major components to your planning: weather and maps.

While others consider talking about the weather as mundane small talk, you'll find the complete opposite for most pilots. Most pilots have a deep sense of weather and are very aware of weather forecasts at all times. One pilot I spoke to even had a weather forecasting station installed on his property. Understandably so, it is no secret that the weather has played a significant role in many aviation accidents.

You'll also need to know how to navigate using a map.

Before heading aloft, you need to pull out the map and plot the trip taking note of visual checkpoints. Though most drivers today rely on GPS to get around when you start out flying you'll learn how to navigate without relying on instruments. You can download a map of your local airspace online, such as on SkyVector.com, and study landmarks that will help you know where you are. If you're someone who always drives by the GPS, turn it off and start getting used to navigating using your surroundings. Pilots who got their training before the GPS was common, fondly speak about the unexpected adventures that came from navigating without one.

Also, side note, if you're like some members of my family and always running your car down to E, know that you won't be able to bring that habit into the cockpit. Unlike driving a car you can't refuel when you feel like it while in the air, so before going you want to make sure that you have enough fuel to reach your destination. If not, you'll want to make sure you identify an airport on the maps where you can plan a refueling stop.

There are many more elements to navigating an airplane, but this was a high-level overview.

Communicate

YOU AVIATE, YOU NAVIGATE, AND lastly, you communicate. Today it's hard to imagine that radios were not a part of the early days of aviation. At first, there was no way to communicate with anyone on the ground or with other aircraft. And if there were multiple people on board they would have to shout over the loud engines. Even when radios were introduced they were often not used during war times because of fear of enemy interception. Today radios are used not only inside the cockpit between pilots but also as a means to communicate throughout the air space with radio towers and other airplanes.

Who, who, where, what

Radio communication is one of the things that most student pilots struggle with. Luckily this is something every pilot has had to face at some point. If the radio was all you had to take into consideration that would be one thing, but you'll have a running machine you're brand new to at your hands and feet.

Most pilots I spoke to admitted that radio communication was one of the most challenging parts of learning how to fly. While some flight instructors said it gets easier after the third or fourth lesson, most pilots said it took a lot more time for them to get really comfortable. "It took the first 20 or 30 hours of flight time to get comfortable speaking on the radios" explains Mike Krass and adds, "Communicating with controllers and other aircraft was incredibly intimidating."

Since radio channels are open for other pilots, your prompts will be kept short and simple to save time and keep the line open for others. Basic radio communication is largely focused on four simple things: who you are speaking to, who you are, where, and what. Let's take an example outside of the cockpit.

You are calling a friend using this format to say what you are doing:
  Who are they: Jerry
  Who are you: Insert your name here
  Where: Insert your location at the moment here
  What: Reading the best book in history

Now that you have the format, let's go over an example from the cockpit:
  Who are they: Los Angeles Tower
  Who are you: Cessna 9962K*
  Where: Holding short of Runway 13
  What: Ready for takeoff

*Unless you're flying for an airline, you use the make and ID number of the aircraft you're in to identify yourself

Radio towers

Broadly speaking there are two types of airports, controlled and uncontrolled. If you fly out of a controlled airport, you'll need to ask air traffic control for permission to move around the airport, take off, and land. How do you know if it's controlled? Look for the tower. You'll refer to it as ATC, which stands for Air Traffic Control. An uncontrolled airport means there is no tower.

For every request you make to ATC, you'll wait for them to respond by repeating your message. They will either be giving your permission to follow through on your request or some other instruction. As you move around the airport you'll be using different channels on your radio. The "hosts" to all these radio channels are Air Traffic Controllers sitting in the Air Traffic Tower, but with different areas they control. They have different responsibilities, but they also act as a team. How many channels there are differs for each airport, but you can find them listed on the airport map, which you can find online for most airports.

The first radio call you have to make is on the Ground radio channel to let them know you're ready to start moving to the runway and also that you've listened to the latest ATIS. ATIS, the abbreviation for Automatic Terminal Information Service, is another channel on your radio that will give the same message over and over again. The message is updated throughout the day but will inform you about the latest weather, cloud cover, and other special notes of what's happening at the airport. If you have ever experienced an interrupted check on your car radio, this is very often what ATIS sounds like. A robot's voice repeats the same message over and over again. Other airports use an actual person.

When you speak to Ground, you'll again follow the pattern "who, who, where, what". Then wait for the Ground radio "host" to let you know further instructions. Once you've heard them, you confirm you have, you start moving towards the runway. Usually Ground will instruct you to stop at a specific point before the runway.

When you arrive at this spot, you let Ground know, again using the same pattern. Before you can take off, you'll need to do the pre-takeoff checklist. Some airports will have a specific area for that, while others less busy airports will let you do it at the beginning of the runway. Once you've completed this checklist, you make your last request to Ground tower, who then tells you to talk to Tower. Once you've completed your final checklist before take-off, you ask the Tower for permission to take off.

If you fly in uncontrolled airspace, you'll still need to report on the radio. But unlike in controlled airspaces you're broadcasting your movements, rather than asking a tower for permission. If there are other pilots around you, you'll have to discuss with them.

Feel like it's a lot to remember? Write the requests and radio frequencies ahead of time. Say it out loud. You can absolutely try to memorize these, but some pilots warned me against it as it might make it harder to perform if there should be any changes. You'll want to focus more on what they're saying, than focusing on if you're sounding cool or not over the radio waves.

If you miss what the tower says, it's also totally ok to ask again. Mike Krass explained: "It's ok to request 'say again' or 'student pilot - say again'. Those are the magic words that will make air traffice controllers slow down, give you instructions in plain English, and make sure that you are fully aware of what is expected of you. Controllers are humans too. Besides they actually don't know who you are, they only know your tail number. They have no idea how many hours you do - or don't - have in your logbook."

Pilot English

To make things a little bit more complicated, this communication is done with the aviation phonetic alphabet and phrases you've probably haven't heard before. Since talking on the radio to announce yourself while doing something you're brand new to, wasn't already intimidating enough. The good news is the international language of flying is English, which I'm assuming you already know since you made it to this point of this book. The bad news is that it still feels like you have to learn a new language, sometimes called "pilot English".

To avoid confusion there is a standard alphabet used on the radio that was put in place across the globe in the 1950s. Instead of saying the letters that identify your aircraft, you'll have to use the aviation phonetic alphabet and numbers. So instead of saying AB192, you'll say Alpha Bravo One Niner Two. You might notice that the nine was said as niner. This is not a typo. This is a tradition that is leftover from back in the day when the radios were filled with static and there was an even higher potential for misunderstandings. The numbers to look out for are three, five, and nine, or in other words: tree, fife, and niner. There are also all sorts of terms that will make you sound like you're starring in a spy movie, like "Roger", "Affirmative", and "Negative contact".

Though everyone is supposed to speak English on the radio, people will deviate from time to time. In my research for my book, I tuned into my local airport in my home country, Norway, and would sometimes hear Norwegian over the line. I also heard from other pilots that the towers often will add their local flair. Some said it is a very common problem for international pilots who fly into the South of Europe because the air towers prefer speaking in their local tongue.

Afraid you'll sound strange? Everyone struggles at the beginning. It helps to realize that every single person on that radio once started from scratch. No one wakes up fluent in radio communication. A great way to practice is to have the alphabet in front of you any time you have to spell something on the phone. Whether you're complaining to your internet provider about your service or telling HR the real spelling of your last name, spell it out using that aviation alphabet:

0	ZE-RO	A	Alpha	N	November
1	WUN	B	Bravo	O	Oscar
2	TOO	C	Charlie	P	Papa
3	TREE	D	Delta	Q	Quebec
4	FOW-er	E	Echo	R	Romeo
5	FIFE	F	Foxtrot	S	Sierra
6	SIX	G	Golf	T	Tango
7	SEV-en	H	Hotel	U	Uniform
8	AIT	I	India	V	Victor
9	NIN-er	J	Juliet	W	Whiskey
		K	Kilo	X	X ray
		L	Lima	Y	Yankee
		M	Mike	Z	Zulu

Another way to practice understanding the radio is to go to LiveAtc.net and find your local airport. If you have no radio experience, I can almost guarantee you won't understand a lot the first time. While doing research for this book, I would listen to the radio for hours. At first, I would jump when the radio barked transmissions after long breaks of silence. Learning to understand what the pilots and towers are saying takes time, but I celebrated the small wins when I understood the words in between. I have made a radio communication Bingo sheet (see below or go to demystiflying.com) that you can use to listen for some words and get that same enjoyment of a micro win.

Instructions: Find your local airport on LiveAtc.net and play bingo. If you want to take this one step further look up the meaning of terms that you don't know.

B	I	N	G	O
"Approach"	Ground	Charlie	"Cleared to land"	"Fife"
"Heavy"	Acknowledge	Someone interrupting someone on the line	"Go around"	"Read back"
"Bravo"	Delta	"Squawk"	"Tower"	"Negative"
"Niner"	"Hold short"	"Affirmative"	"Line up and wait"	"Fly heading"
"Say again"	"Verify"	Painful static from someone's radio	"Cleared for takeoff"	"Alpha"

Having spoken to really accomplished pilots and knowing they started the same way was comforting. Yes, they might be captains of big flight teams today, but one time they were also nervous and were worried everyone on the radio heard their mistake. I got the chance to speak to a former ATC controller who admits it's harder to be the one requesting permission than being the one who gives orders. He told me it is intimidating to be on the pilot side.

One pilot I spoke to said there is no such thing as a good radio talker. "My grandfather who's flown professionally his entire life will still frequently come back from flying and share embarrassing stories of how he said the wrong thing". It doesn't matter if you are 16, 50, or 75 years old with no experience or a lot of it, everyone will make mistakes on the radio from time to time.

Squawk

Though it often feels like the people who work at an air control tower are some super-powered creatures from a different world who can hear and see everything on the ground and in the air, I have to disappoint*. These are humans that also started one day like you not knowing their aviation alphabet or what radio channels to tune into. They do however have a trick up their sleeve that helps in their observation that you as a student pilot will not have, the squawks.

Squawk is the old-school version of sharing your location with someone on your phone. The way you give ATC permission to track you is by typing a string of numbers into a little box in your aircraft, called the transponder. When you are starting off learning how to fly this code is 1200. The transponder will with this code send a signal to the airport's own radar and show up on a map that the ATC guy or girl can access. So when you practice listening to the radio and you hear someone being called out it is because ATC can see their squawk. There are also some codes that are designed to be used in case of emergency.

*After having gotten the chance to visit a tower as a part of my research I will say that it sometimes feels like they see everything, and they do. The 360 view of the airport gives them full insight into what goes on in the nearby airspace and runways. That could possibly be called a superpower after all.

And that was a general overview of how to aviate, navigate and communicate. Of course, you won't be able to go flying solely on that information alone, but hopefully, you feel better prepared for what a pilot's journey entails. Yes, it seems like a lot, but I hope you can see that through a little bit of effort, you too can fly.

CHAPTER FOUR

Flying isn't free

ONE FACTOR THAT DETRACTS A lot of people from getting their pilot license is the sticker shock. Flying is not a cheap skill to learn. But why is flying so expensive? The training has a lot of different required expenses to it and it all adds up. Add additional training needed to understand a concept or the time it takes to relearn after a break you see an even higher number on the bottom line. The two main costs, excluding fees, ground school, books, and other miscellaneous costs, are instruction and rental costs. The goal of this chapter is to explore some of the ways others have funded their pilot license and some free things one can do outside the cockpit to become a better pilot.

There are two different running meters once you show up to your flight lessons. The first "meter" belongs to your instructor. Obviously, your instructor expects to be paid for the time he or she spends with you. This time starts ticking from the moment your lesson begins, which most of the time will not be by the aircraft, to the end of your class. The second meter is an actual meter that's called the Hobbs meter. This meter starts ticking as soon as the engine of the airplane is turned on to you switch it off. So even if you only spent 20 minutes in the air, but hung out with your instructor for 2 hours, both are added to your total costs of that lesson.

The most obvious way around this monetary hurdle is to get someone else to pay for it. Or even better, get paid to fly. The only way to get paid while learning from scratch is through the military. Now keep in mind joining the military doesn't guarantee you a pilot's license. It's a competitive world and each branch has its own evaluations on who gets to get those wings and who doesn't.

No two pilots' journey is the same. You might already have the money available today or you might have to find other ways to fund your pilot license. Most pilots I spoke to did not originally have the means to fund their pilot license. They all had to work hard to find ways to make it happen. The silver lining of these stories was often the unexpected opportunities that arose along the way.

Jim Anderson's story is a great example. He found multiple ways of funding his training, including student loans, working at the flight school for hours and lessons, and washing their airplanes. "I ended up not having a car for a while, lived in a very low-cost rented mobile home, and had a scooter, but owned an older Cessna 172. Aviation is not cheap, never has been, but if there is a will there's away. Sounds rough right? Sure, sacrifices were made, but would not have done it any differently knowing what I know now. Looking back, rising to the occasion and not giving up on a goal you are passionate about gave me more of a life lesson rather than just a pilot certificate. The pilot certificate was a bonus!"

Let's go over an example of what to expect from a local flight school. Let's assume your flight instructor Mary charges $90 an hour. Most lessons are going to run on average for two hours. This includes some review with your instructor, performing the pre-flight review of the airplane, time in the air, and wrap-up. Mary's rate is therefore multiplied by 2 hours, which means she gets paid $180 for her time. However, this does not factor in the added cost of what it cost to rent the airplane. Remember the Hobbs meter? Since you only pay for the time you're using the airplane, aka when the Hobbs meter is running, you most likely have less than the time spent with an instructor. Let's say the airplane was running for 20 mins and the hourly rental is $150, you will pay $50 for the aircraft rental. Some places will charge additionally for the fuel, while others will include the fuel in the hourly rental rate. A lot of times you'll see the hourly rate listed with the word wet in parenthesis, which means fuel is included in the price.

Keep in mind that the FAA requires you to have 40 hours in the air to be able to take the final exam for your private license. Two things about that: one, most people need more time to build the confidence and skill to be able to complete that final check ride. Two, the hours are counted excludes the time you've spent with your instructor on the ground, it only counts the time you've been in the air. Which your friend, the Hobbs meter (or in some cases the Tachometer), will be helpful in telling you.

You'll get to know the Hobbs meter quickly when you start flying, so you might as well get to know it now. Think of it as an old-school punch card machine for the aircraft: a running meter that can measure how long an aircraft is in use. The Hobbs meter was invented in the late 1930s and is named after the man who invented it, John Weston Hobbs. Yay, it's not another abbreviation! Lawyers charge for their time in increments of 15 minutes. Similarly, the Hobbs meter records your flying time in one-tenth of an hour. On top of being the most common way rental costs are calculated, this is the measure you'll use to record your flight hours in your logbook.

Another meter you'll get to know as you start your training is the Tachometer. Personally, I wish the tachometer was a measure for how many tacos I eat every year, but in reality, it measures Tach time. It's pronounced tack-o-meter. Tach time measures how many turns the engine needs to keep up with the speed you are flying, or in other words the tachometer measures the revolutions per minute (RPM). An easier way to remember might be knowing that the word derives from the Greek words "tachos", meaning speed, and "metron", meaning measure. The tachometer is also used as an indicator to determine when the aircraft needs maintenance. If you're into expensive watches, the tachymeter on your Rolex is not the same as a tachometer.

Just like the Hobbs meter, you'll want to write down the Tachometer before and after each flight in the airplane's own logbook. It might seem like a time-saving shortcut to use the tachometer for your logbook, but you'll actually end up logging less flight time in your logbook. Some say there is a 20% difference in the time logged with the Hobbs meter and Tachometer.

Prices of the aircraft rental will vary based on the cost it requires a flight school to run, which includes the cost to rent space, maintenance, and local salaries. The same goes for the hourly cost of the instructor. For that reason, as you might expect prices are going to be more expensive in the bigger cities, and lower in less populated areas. If you're taking lessons at a busy airport, for example in New York or Los Angeles, you also might find that you're paying extra to wait for commercial traffic. On the other hand, I'm not going to lie, it's kind of awesome to be in a small plane waiting behind a Delta plane about to take off.

I will repeat myself: If you find schools that promise you your license at an extremely low cost, please don't proceed. If it's too good to be true, it probably is. There are ways for schools to lower their rates, but few that are acceptable for your own safety.

Like previously mentioned, flying is a perishable skill. The number one stealer of both time and money in aviation is learning gaps. You are actually better off flying several times a week as opposed to one. You'll spend more money by flying once a week because most of us will have a hard time retaining complex concepts without frequent repetition with a short time in between. And when you forget what you've learned, you'll most likely spend additional time with your instructor relearning that information. I am one who had to learn that hard way. The confidence in my ability and knowledge waned quickly, despite having a lesson only a few days earlier. And at my next lesson, I had to pay for extra instruction time to ensure my understanding was still correct.

Rescheduling of lessons is bound to happen, which will potentially result in even more days between your lessons. Weather cancel flights everywhere. Even in sunny California, we have the marine layer. In Florida, they are challenged with thunderstorms. If you have more lessons every week, it won't be such a big deal if one class gets canceled. And of course, don't forget to prepare ahead for your lessons, both by reviewing your past lesson and studying what is on the agenda for your next.

As helicopter and airplane pilot, Jaden Risner, puts it: "Be as consistent as possible with your training - as large breaks between your lessons will extend your training time having to review and warm-up and ultimately cost you more money. As someone who worked several jobs as a young teen to pay for my flight lessons, this was always a challenge."

Free introductory flight

You might be able to get your free flight lesson for free! In 1992, the Experimental Aircraft Association (EAA) introduced the Young Eagles program in the US. Thanks to over 40,000 volunteer Young Eagles pilots, anyone in age 8-17 years old can apply for their first ride in an airplane free of charge. A few years later they introduced the Eagles program for those of us who are older than 18 years old. Both of the programs are designed to give someone a taste of flying through a one-time demonstration flight and support them with resources to get their license.

Scholarships

Due to the ongoing looming pilot shortage, there are a lot of resources available to help prospective pilots with the financial challenge of how to fund their pilot training. There are also a lot of pilots out there who love flying so much and are keen to see other people get their chance in the cockpit. The combination of these two translates into lots of scholarships available.

There is no official number of how many, but there are many in a wide area of categories, including general training, regional, minority, and college scholarships. Even if you don't want to become a professional pilot, there are also a lot of different scholarships available to hobby pilots.

A few years ago, flight instructor and Jet Blue Pilot, Carl Valeri, was inspired by his mother helping people in their local community apply for college. He wanted to do something to help both aspiring and experienced pilots and decided to make a scholarship guide. So with the help of his mother, Valeri, created *The Aerospace Scholarships*, which included scholarships for about $50,000.

Unfortunately, Carl's mother passed in the midst of its development, but Valeri could hear her voice saying "You can do better" and continue to push through to improve the guide. Today the scholarships guide includes over 200 Aerospace scholarships with a combined value of over $120 Million. And the guide is updated regularly to assure accuracy. "The only thing that holds people back from getting scholarships is that they don't apply", explains Valeri. "Every year there are many scholarships that don't get dispersed because there were no applicants". If you are pursuing a college degree, you might also want to check out the general scholarship guides that are available for all students. And make sure to check with your school to see what financial aid packages they offer.

Sometimes scholarships are awarded for beginner pilots, but they're also awarded to help pilots progress in their careers. Sarah Tamar. Kohan, a seaplane pilot, was one of those who received a scholarship recently to pursue her certified instructor license (CFI). She was awarded the *Women In Aviation/Martha R. King Scholarship* donated by the King School. "I applied because the CFI is a huge goal of mine and my next step in my aviation career. The Kings are amazing and the scholarship absolutely changed my life."

Scholarships aren't just the case in the U.S. UK-based Grace McKellar is a future commercial pilot and host of her own podcast *Beyond the Cockpit*. She was awarded *The British Women Pilot's Association (BWPA) Flight Deck Wingman Scholarship* in the spring of 2021 to help develop the skills she needs to secure her first job as a commercial pilot. "It's really really exciting", she says about this new start after feeling she had been out of the loop due to COVID and airline furloughs. And she was one of 19 pilots that BWPA was able to financially help along with their pilot goals.

Financing

There are plenty of financing options out there. Before you get a loan to finance your pilot license I would suggest knowing why you are getting into aviation. Generally speaking, invest in education and use money that you already have for fun. If you want to get your private pilot license as a bucket list item, I would highly suggest starting a savings account to reach that goal.

If your goal is to fly professionally and you don't have the needed funds, loans might be the only way. I'm not a financial advisor, but I have to issue a warning. Make sure you read those terms and don't commit before you know what you're getting into. Blue skies can quickly become dark clouds if you get in financial trouble.

Airline training programs

Another common type of financing is to get training costs covered by the airlines. Due to a pilot shortage, European airlines started funding the pilot training. In recent years, U.S.-based airlines have followed suit. The application requirements vary for each program. Some allow candidates to join without any prior experience, others expect some prior training.

The longest-running airline program in the U.S., Jet Blue Gateway Select, partners with aviation universities and flight school and provide a career development program for their selected cadets. The program provides financing options, training, and a time-building program which eventually results in job placement at Jet Blue.

In 2022, United Airlines took it further and launched its very own academy called United Aviate Academy in Phoenix, Arizona. While the other programs typically train their candidates through partner schools and colleges, this Academy has its own fleet of airplanes and instructors. In order to apply, you will need to have completed high school or have a GED diploma. Once accepted, United will cover the training required for your private pilot license, but you will have to pay roughly $70,000 for the advanced training. Once you graduate, you'll be placed with a United Airlines regional partner to get the required hours you need to become a first officer with United.

So what's the catch? One of the common setups is that the training is provided in a form of a loan. The airline will expect you to pay it down while you work for them. Should you decide to quit or have a change of heart, you're still on the hook for the financial investment the company made on you. Some airline programs also might require a certain required amount of years with them before you're allowed to work for another airline. But if you know that you want to become an airline pilot, it offers excellent training and is the closest to what can be considered a job placement guarantee in the industry.

Work, work, work

One of my favorite parts of my research was hearing the creative ways people found to pay for their pilot training. It's inspiring how people find ways to finance their dreams. And how these creative ways often led to open doors that hadn't been there before. An example from the early days of aviation is Bessie Coleman. Coleman grew up in Texas in the 1900s and was interested in flying from a young age. Flight training was not offered to women in the U.S. at the time, but that didn't discourage Coleman. She worked multiple jobs and saved the money to move to France to get her license there. In 1920, she arrived in France only knowing basic French and in June 1921, she became the first African American and Native American woman to have a pilot license.

I heard many similar stories in my interviews. Commercial

pilots would share stories of how they got their break into aviation. Some of these jobs included washing airplanes, working as mechanics, refueling aircraft, and customer service at local charter companies. Pilots would tell me how they were able to absorb information outside of the cockpit by being in proximity. Being at the airport you get acquainted with the airport culture and that has some perks.

When Ryan Riley was 14 years old he went to the local airport asking for flight lessons not realizing how expensive flying was. He subsequently asked for a job but was told they didn't hire kids. Determined, Riley came back every Friday afternoon week after week to ask again before the airfield manager eventually relented. First, he was assigned the painstakingly difficult job of repainting the beacon tower, probably as a test to scare him off. When it didn't, he got put to wash and refuel airplanes and over time given more and more responsibilities around the airport. In return, he got paid in discounted lessons and academic books.

At 17, he not only had his pilot license but he was nicknamed the Deputy Airfield Manager and would often be put in charge of the whole airport when the Airfield Manager had to be away for a few days. Riley laughed recalling those moments "He would say "Don't break anything while I'm gone."" Riley's story is one that shows the importance of perseverance, which he brought with him into his career in the U.S. Air Force, where he eventually became one of the few pilots that have made it into the legendary Thunderbird Demonstration Squadron.

Airline pilot, Jessica Wolcott, didn't have the means to pursue a pilot degree at a college. "I worked in customer service at a flight school and got discounted flight lessons while earning money," explained Wolcott. In addition to getting discounted rates for flight lessons, she was able to make connections she wouldn't have been able to build elsewhere. Another pilot who worked at his local airport told me if he was lucky how other pilots would let him fly with them after his shift. Someone he worked with met another pilot that was so kind to let him borrow his aircraft.

Many airline pilots will continue to have other jobs even after they work for the airlines. There are a lot of ups and downs in the airline industry and it's a way to keep control of time and money beyond one employer. United Airlines pilot and flight instructor, Tanner Harris, started a drone imaging services company, Blue Nose Aerial, at the beginning of the pandemic when the need for training pilots had quickly come to a halt. "It's opened up avenues into other parts of the aviation world and provided financial stability in a dynamic and sometimes volatile airline industry," he explains.

Honing your skills outside the cockpit
You can save many hours in learning (or relearning) new concepts in the comfort of your home. The more you practice your skills outside of flight training, the more you can make of your paid instruction time. Here are some ways to become free (or close to free) ways to hone pilot skills outside the cockpit:

You can read it or pay for the teaching
One common mistake student pilots make is thinking that it's the flight instructor's responsibility to ensure they understand the concepts. The idea is that you are paying for the hours so obviously they should spend "your" time with them explaining everything. Even though studying can be tough (and at times reaaaal boring), understanding the concepts outside of the cockpit without your instructor is not only going to make you a better pilot, but it will also save you money in the long run. "You can read it or pay for the teaching," Brian E. Miller told me (more like shouted because

he was interrupted by planes taking off).

Speaking to flight instructors all over the world, I heard over and over again that the most successful lessons were the ones where the student came prepared. You're not going to be able to understand most concepts by only reading about them. However, when you study, you'll help shorten the distance between your brain and physical actions. Flying is a lot about building muscle memory. And by studying ahead of time, you'll increase the chances of learning concepts fully.

Accomplished pilots would tell me that studying never ends. After you get your license, the studying transforms into preparation for flights. French-Canadian former fighter jet pilot, Pierre-Henri "ATÉ" Chuet, told me the more you advance the bigger the need to over-prepare. On his popular YouTube video, you can see how he now adapts aviation proven methods beyond the cockpit as a global keynote speaker.

One instructor I spoke to suggested doing the written exam before you start flight training, while another suggested getting some hours in the cockpit before starting to study. If you're already set on and super passionate about getting into the cockpit, the first one might be good for you. There are benefits to getting your written exam out of the way. Having completed the theory makes it easier for both the student and the instructor because there is a strong foundation of knowledge.

However, if you're like me, who had never been in a cockpit when I first showed up at the airport, studying might be a deterrent rather than a money saver. If I was told I had to read Anna Karenina or any other massively large classic work of literature as an introduction to reading books, I probably wouldn't have been the fan I am of reading today. For some of us, it makes sense to have a small taste of what we're getting into, before taking the full dive.

Memorizing checklists

While interviewing pilots, I got to speak to military pilots from all over the world. A unique aspect of their training I quickly came to learn was the requirement to memorize everything. Checklists, procedures, and manuals, you have to know it all by heart. "We're expected to know the checklist by heart. During my training, I went from not knowing anything to a point where I was able to spit out the checklists in my sleep" Red Bull pilot and Norwegian military pilot, Eskil Amdal, told me. He explained how memorizing normal and emergency procedures allow you to bring more situational awareness when you're flying.

Though military pilots aren't expected to go over checklists without reading them, the thought is the knowledge is so ingrained in their minds they don't need to. If you become a pilot outside the military, you will always be expected to read the lists out loud. However, the added benefit of memorization is still there. Knowing the checklists word by word will make you more confident and you will be able to stay ahead mentally.

Chair flying

When I started taking flying lessons, I didn't actually believe that people used chair flying as a training tool. Boy, was I wrong? We went over chair flying earlier, but a refresher never hurts. You sit in a chair and go through each and every step of a flight. If you want to see chair flying in action, I recommend going to YouTube and looking up the video called "Take a look inside of the Blue Angels briefing room". You'll see the legendary U.S. Navy Demonstration team plan as they conduct a chairfly brief before a flight show.

What is great about chairflying is that you can fly your entire lesson on the ground. "Similar to sports, creating your flight ahead of time and envisioning every single step will allow you to focus on the contingencies that come up," explains San Diego based pilot Jaden Risner. "Even better, find a partner or someone to do it with you and challenge each other to fly it to perfection before your flight."

I was also surprised to learn that all over the world, military pilots were given pictures of cockpits to hang up on a wall and practice. Fighter pilot at Royal Canadian Air-force, Renaud "Grat" Thys, spoke with me from Newfoundland, Canada, about when he started flight school. He was given a poster of the inside of the airplane he was training in. "You can go over checklists and procedures with all the buttons of the cockpit in front of you. Doing this will help with your workload in the cockpit. Your knowledge will go from conscious to subconscious." He recently messaged me to tell me he just started training for another type of jet. And with a new jet, a new poster went up on his wall.

Even though you're not in the military, you can do this at home. Thanks to the good ol' internet you can find high-resolution images of pretty much any cockpit out there. Once you know what kind of aircraft you'll be training in, you can find it and print it out. Hang the poster up on your wall, grab a chair, and start chair-flying.

Want to take your chair flying even further? Mike Krass suggests: "Tune your handheld radio into a busy frequency. I usually pick Atlanta, Minneapolis, LAX, or Dallas-Ft Worth. Pretend you are one of the call signs (Delta 11 heavy, for example) and follow all the instructions the controller gives that aircraft. Plus, then you get the pretend like you're flying a Delta 777!" Krass further explains how chair flying allows you to simulate the maneuvers and also memorize the procedures.

Simulators

Flying simulators isn't just the entertainment of teenage boys, but a legit way to learn the controls of a cockpit without paying an instructor. Military pilot programs all over the world have started using simulators and virtual reality as a part of their training. Instead of starting training in the cockpit, the training is now started in a digital reality.

For a lot longer, airlines across the globe have sent their pilots both to learn and maintain their skills in simulators. Before any pilot gets the chance to sit in the seat of a commercial airliner, they train hours and hours in a simulator. I once had to chance to simulate a Gulfstream G5 at Flight Safety in Los Angeles and I can tell you how quickly you forget it is not the real thing. My terrible (crash) landing in virtual Las Vegas felt very much real. Both mentally and physically. These simulators are however very expensive and not for private use. But there are many low-cost alternatives that can make a better pilot from the comfort of your home. The most common software is the Microsoft Flight Simulator, which has been around since the 70s. "The 2020 version is so accurate. It's so good!" Sumner Lee, a retired U.S. Navy pilot, told me when I asked him of things one could do outside the cockpit to become a better pilot. The Microsoft program gives anyone the ability to simulate the experience of flying in a multitude of different aircraft and locations. There are, of course, other aviation simulation software out there, but Microsoft is the oldest and most well-known. The aspiring airline pilot, Alaya Dyson, is a fan of this form of studying and suggests adding equipment to go along with the software, such as rudder pedals. "You can find this on eBay or Amazon. This helps with practicing at home," Dyson says.

Hang(ar) around

Want to learn for free and be social at the same time? Most of the pilots I interviewed talked passionately about how they built skills outside of flight hours by hanging out at the local airport. Some could tell me their best friendships have been forged by hanging out in the hangars. "They say if you want to catch a cold, get around sick people. I made sure I was around people who were smarter than me and would ask lots of questions. I found that people are able to break down concepts that I found hard to understand from textbooks," flight instructor David Gibbons told me.

It's hard to have access to a plethora of pilots and hangar time if one is new to this world, but don't worry. Hit up the observer deck at your local airport. Not only will you be able to see landings and take-offs, but you can see many different kinds of aircraft. Beyond learning the lingo, there is confidence built-in recognizing a Boing 737 or being able to call out that is a G6. The decks are usually filled with other aviation enthusiasts. Some because they fly themselves, some because they used to fly and some that are just obsessed with aircraft as flying machines. Oklahoma-based flight instructor, Collin Craytor, encourages anyone interested in flying to hang out at the airport. "You never know who you will meet and what you will get to fly. Small airports across the country are filled with wonderful people that have interesting airplanes!"

A pro tip is to listen to the local air control tower while you're there. Go to LiveAtc.net and find your tower. Don't know what the tower is called? This is a great conversation starter to ask someone else at the observer deck. Listening to the air traffic control tower is comparable to adding subtitles to a foreign film. Anyone who's told you that they've learned a language knows how helpful the captions are to the images presented on the screen.

Another way to meet other pilots is to go to a local Experimental Aircraft Association (EAA) chapter meeting.

"Other social groups are out there as well, but EAA speaks to a wide range of aviators and the chapters usually have some very interesting members who are all happy to share experience and knowledge," says Jim Anderson. EAA is one of the largest aviation organizations in the world and has local chapters all over the U.S. and Canada.

Working out
Working out isn't just positive for your health and overall well-being, but it can help you in the cockpit. Instructor Pilot and Combat Aviation advisor for the U.S. Air Force Special Operations Command, Beau Suder, recounted how flying can be taxing on the body. One of his top advice to make you a better pilot outside the cockpit was to invest time in both physical and mindset training. "When your body and mind calm down, you can bring this calmness to training and flying overall and better fall back on your training," he explains.

Free resources
There might not be such a thing as a free lunch but there is the internet. And it's filled with many free resources available to make studying and understanding easier. There is a sense of envy from pilots who trained before the internet was around. Jim Anderson wrote me "..most of the books I had to purchase years ago are available as free downloads today".
Here is a list of some free resources you can find online:

- The "boss of aviation" itself, Federal Aviation, has a website with many available resources on FAASafety.gov.
- Another great resource is AOPA.org, Aircraft Owners and Pilots Association (AOPA)'s website. They also offer a 6-month free membership, which includes a monthly magazine.
- You can find a whole list of helpful content on

EAA.com. This is the website for Experimental Aircraft Association (EAA), which also offers free introductory flights to aspiring pilots.

- Don't forget about the library! Either your local library or some of the free online ones online. Some of the best aviation books are the ones that were written long before flying became mainstream.
- Another obvious resource is YouTube. Type in anything you'll ever wonder and I bet you someone has made a video explaining it. I'll warn you sometimes you'll get a little dizzy watching amateur video, but the passion these pilots have outweighs that.

I'll be the first one to say that sometimes pilot resources can be a little intimidating for a non-pilot. When you don't speak pilot it might take more time to understand. But always try reading or watching something one more time to understand before you move on. And write down terms and look them up. I promise you with time, you'll start picking up these terms quicker and quicker until it feels natural.

You now have a better understanding of how to fund your license and some ways to save time and money in the process. But before you start the training, make sure you have your personal finances squared away. How you decide to pay for your training, is on you. All I'm saying is to have a plan of attack before you get started. Unfortunately, it's very common for people to get started without an end goal in mind and find that it is going to take them more time and money than they expected.

Having thought through this ahead of time will help you make the necessary decisions you will have to make easier. So when you start your training make sure you have an overview of your expected hours and try to stick to that as much as possible. Be confident to speak up if you're not sure about a certain topic, but also do your best to study outside of school. And don't forget to apply for scholarships!

CHAPTER FIVE

Co-pilot

WHILE THE MERE ACT OF becoming a pilot is a solo journey, having someone to debrief with along your journey can make the process a lot better. Knowing that you can call someone with who you're not in a paid relationship (as you technically are in with your instructor) can be extremely beneficial. This person can be key when meeting learning challenges or when you're facing a plateau in your training. Your very own co-pilot.

In conversations with military pilots, there is no doubt that there is an added benefit of having a group alongside your journey. When speaking to Andy Christopher, retired U.S. Navy pilot, he shared with me: "We were twelve starting out together. There was an incredible bond formed as we were cooperating to graduate." Again and again, I would hear military pilots echo his description of this camaraderie. A camaraderie that blossomed after helping each other through long grueling days during flight training. Friendships were made despite an awareness that there was an underlying competition in place.

The importance of a community is also recognized at colleges and airline pilot program schools. Michael Wildes, a former flight instructor with Embry-Riddle, explained, "At first you start college wanting to prove yourself as the best pilot among your peers. But through the years you see friendships formed amongst the students and that they get the benefit of working together." As students mature they start seeing the benefit of learning alongside others rather than comparing themselves to each other.

No comparison allowed

As you find new friends in the pilot community, it can be easy to fall into the trap of comparing your skills to theirs. Some of the students you're surrounded by may be further ahead. When I asked legendary acrobatic pilot, Patty Wagstaff, what the most challenging part of learning how to fly was for her, she replied "Realizing that everyone starts somewhere." But just like in life you shouldn't compare yourself, focus on yourself. Stay in your own lane, and concentrate on learning.

Use your new friends as a source of motivation. Personally, I loved hearing about the best flying experiences that pilots have had, and picture myself in their shoes. It's probably too late for me to join the military and land a fighter jet on a carrier out in the ocean, but no one can stop me from dreaming.

Retired U.S. Navy pilot, Knight Campbell, made me daydream about flying into the sunset: "We were flying off the coast of Malaysia somewhere. It was sunset. Just because of the way the atmosphere goes, there was this giant red sun. It was really, really cool. And then there was an eclipse! We had no idea that this was going to happen. The size of the sky, this ridiculously large red sun with an eclipse. Then it hit us, if we climb, we can watch this for longer. So we just kept climbing and then the sun kept going down. And we got to watch this amazing sunset eclipse."

Get to know other pilots

Don't know any pilots yet? Luckily pilots love talking about aviation, so finding connections in this space isn't difficult. When I became interested in flying I knew only one pilot. But ever since I started this project, pilots from all over the world have welcomed me. Sumner Lee, a retired Naval Aviator and founder of Fuse Integration, described it as "a community that looks out for each other." He shared many stories of pilots helping each other, from the beginner levels to the more advanced stages.

Here are some quick ways to find pilot friends:
- Ask your friends and family if they know any pilots. You'll be surprised to discover how many people actually know a pilot when you start looking! Believe me, I know.
- Scan your social media platforms:
- look for individuals on LinkedIn by searching pilots
- join groups online
- search your local airport's location on Instagram to identify some local pilots
- Go to your local airport. If showing up at someone's hangar when you don't know them isn't your cup of tea (it ain't mine), start by going to the local observation deck.
- Join a local club. The extent of a flying club varies, but most of them charge a fee. Some host monthly meetings to create a community, while others own planes as a group. AOPA has a club finder on their website.
- Ask at your local flight school if they know anyone who's interested in having a study buddy or wanting to form a study group.
- Attend ground school. Both through virtual and in-

person ground schools, you are likely to meet others who are on a similar stage as you in their pilot journey.

- Lastly, just tell everyone you know that you are working on your pilot license, I guarantee the most lovely, unexpected connections and experiences will come from it. And who knows it might lead to long-term friendships.

Jonathan Rosenthal grew up biking over to Van Nuys Airport in Los Angeles and was daydreaming about being a pilot. Seeing his son's passion for airplanes, his mother suggested he reach out to the local radio station, KNBC. She had a hunch that the radio's pilot who made the daily traffic reports might not mind the company of a kid in the cockpit. Rosenthal took his mother's advice to heart and wrote a letter to the radio station. Not long after he got an invitation to go flying.

The KNBC helicopter pilot turned out to be Francis Gary Powers. Powers now working a comparatively normal job was an aviator legend. Before starting on the radio he had gotten known for being a pilot of the CIA and being aboard a spy plane that was shot down while on a surveillance mission in the Soviet Union Airspace. This experience solidified Rosenthal's own dream and he went on to get his own license at an age of 16. Later on, he would also successfully launch, NetAir, a nationwide jet taxi service. NetAir went on to become the largest charter jet company in the U.S. None of this might have happened had he not shared his dream with the people around him.

Maybe you already have a friend who's also interested in becoming a pilot who you can convince to join you? Sharing a common hobby is a great way to stay connected to a good friend, and it can also be helpful in the journey to have someone who understands what you're going through.

Additionally, there is the added benefit of learning by watching someone else in the process. U.S. Air Force pilot, Michael Krysinski, learned alongside his friend for his private pilot license before he joined the military. The two would split the hour lesson in two and have 30 minutes each at the controls. The other one could sit back and observe and learn from the other's successes and mistakes.

Your logbook will still officially only give you the time you were in control in the cockpit. For instance, if you flew for 30 minutes you'll only be able to use 30 minutes towards the 40 hours requirement. But this way you'll be able to study alongside someone and be able to observe someone doing the very same things you were learning.

Back in early aviation days before airplanes were standardized, flight schools wouldn't let students touch in the cockpit the first two weeks of training. For the initial time, their only job was to observe and learn. Today that is less common of practice, much of it because of the high cost of flight training. But sharing the cockpit with a friend makes that possible. Students who go through full-time flight programs and the military talk about the benefit of partnering. Beyond the support of a friend, you will also have someone that can challenge you and you can debrief with after the lessons.

A co-pilot is not required

There are plenty of pilots I spoke to who made it through without anyone close to their side. These pilots would often find comfort and inspiration in reading about others in aviation.

HISTORIC FIGURES

Sharon Preszler had to navigate her U.S. Air Force experience surrounded by mostly men. She didn't really have anyone she could look to who had done the same before her. She had to carve the unknown journey ahead on her own. Though she didn't have someone's journey to trace, she did find inspiration to stick through the toughest days by reading about other aviators, including the WASP.

The WASP was, not an insect or group of rich people in the 80s, but an incredible group of women who flew airplanes during World War 2. These 1,100 Women Air Force Service Pilots were essential in the war. They transported planes, trained new pilots, and would often also be test pilots. All of this was done as civilians, they were never officially recognized as a military organization though they played key roles in important missions. This meant they didn't get the same benefits as their male peers who were in the military. These brave women often risked their own lives, but still had to pay for their own uniforms and transport to and from their assignments.

These WASP women were finally officially celebrated in 2009 when given the Congressional Medal by President Barack Obama when he said: "The Women Air Force Service Pilots courageously answered their country's call in a time of need while blazing a trail for the brave women who have given and continue to give so much in service to this nation since. Every American should be grateful for their service, and I am honored to sign this bill to finally give them some of the hard-earned recognition they deserve."

Inspired by these women, Preszler went on to become the first female to fly the F-16. The F-16, full name General Dynamics F-16 Fighting Falcon, is often nicknamed "Viper" among pilots, because of its similarities to a viper snake. This fighter jet has room for one pilot and has a top speed of about 1,300 mph. That's closer to seven times the top speed of a Ferrari. Translation: that's fast.

IF THEY DID, YOU CAN TOO

From other areas of my life, I've realized that you don't have
to actually know someone for them to be an inspiration.
Sometimes all we need is to see that someone else has forged
the path in front of us. Maybe they have another aspect of
their life that reminds us of our own path. Here is a list of
some noteworthy people who got their licenses. If they did,
you can too:

  Michael Bloomberg
  Jimmy Buffet
  Gisele Bundchen
  Tom Cruise
  Roald Dahl
  Bruce Dickinson
  Clint Eastwood
  King Willem-Alexander
  Larry Ellison
  Harrison Ford
  Morgan Freeman
  Craig Ferguson
  Angelina Jolie
  Tim McGraw
  Phil Mickelson
  Elon Musk
  Brad Pitt
  Kurt Russell
  Evan Spiegel
  Hillary Swank
  John Travolta

BOOKS

One of my favorite parts of doing research for this book was
reading about aviators. Not only was it inspiring to read
what others were thinking as they were training to be pilots,

but it was also a great way to learn about the world in the skies.

Every author has a way of explaining aviation concepts and you naturally get the benefit of immersion into aviation through different perspectives. There is beauty in seeing the same terms repeated in different stories, and it also deepens your understanding. Reading books will not replace ground school and actual flight training, but it will help you grasp many different concepts. Here are some of my favorites:

The Early History of the Airplane - The Wright Brothers
Fate is the Hunter - Ernest Gann
Fly Girls - Keith O'Brien
Going Solo - Roald Dahl
Jonathan Livingston Seagull - Richard Bach
Stick and Rudder - Wolfgang Langewiesche
The Curtiss Aviation Book - Glenn Hammond Curtiss
The Story of American Aviation - James G. Ray
West with the Night - Beryl Markham
Who Were the Tuskegee Airmen - Sherri L. Smith
Wind, Sand, and Stars - Antoine de Saint-Exupery

As you know by now, I never get tired of hearing what originally inspired people to become pilots. Hearing the starting point of this common dream before embarking on the path was almost as inspiring as hearing about their flight journeys. Many men and women were inspired by watching Tom Cruise and Val Kilmer flying jets in Top Gun and then decided to go chase their dream. Flight crew servicing passengers in the airplane cabin decided to not just dream about flying the airplane but ended up doing it. Kids who had seen an airplane or helicopter grace the sky and decided that "one day that will be me."

After the Vietnam war, the military was struggling with their recruitment. Many different marketing

tactics were attempted to get the attention of young men and women, but without doubt, there was one tactic that was more successful than the others. The U.S. Navy collaborated with Hollywood to create Top Gun with Tom Cruise and Val Kilmer at the TOPGUN Academy. In reality, the movie was not only a box office success, but the recruitment rates were up 500% in the following year. From my interviews, it is obvious that the movie inspired many to become pilots for decades after.

Bjørn Kjos grew up with a dad that owned a small airline company in a little town in Norway. But it wasn't his dad's journey alone that inspired him, it was the vision of a local man who came flying over their farm in his jet while on leave from the military. Later he himself joined the Norwegian Air Force and became a pilot. He attended TOPGUN school in the U.S. as a part of his training. "It was really, really fast", he lights up in our interview when he remembered his first flight in a fighter jet. Eventually, he did end up going in his dad's footsteps and establishing his own airline, Norwegian Airlines. Norwegian Airlines despite coming out of a small country is today one of the largest European airlines.

Kenyatta Ruffin was only five years old when he decided he wanted to become an astronaut. Not shy to tell anyone about his dream, his community started pitching in to help him achieve it. He was only 14 years old when he flew a glider solo. "I received a lot of support, a ton of support, and I wouldn't have gotten to where I am today had it not been for that." Today, Ruffin is not only an accomplished Air Force fighter pilot and a White House Fellow but is committed to paying it forward. He founded the Legacy Flight Academy™ (LFA), a non-profit focused on helping minorities and underrepresented youth achieve success in aerospace and STEM careers.

Don't have the same career clarity as 5-year-old Ruffin? For some, the path towards flying has been written along the way. One of the most legendary female pioneers in aviation history is an example of this. Jackie Cochran started working at the age of 8 years old out of necessity and worked her way up to become a sought-after hairstylist in New York and Miami. At 26, she told her future husband, Floyd Bostwick Odlum, her dream of starting her own traveling cosmetics company. He jokingly responded then she would need to become a pilot. Cochran ended up getting her license not long after.

Her pilot classes were paid by Odlum because he lost their bet: that she wouldn't be able to get her license in less than three months. Cochran managed it after just 2.5 weeks. From that moment on, Cochran made a name in both the business world and in the world of aviation. She became the first woman to exceed the speed of sound. She was also the person who convinced the military to set up the female pilot group who assisted during World War 2, the WASP. At one point she had more world records in aviation than any man or woman.

These doors that opened from people's pilot journeys were so many. New friends, marriages, job opportunities, book deals, and unforgettable travels. Not a single pilot I spoke to was able to predict these outcomes from that first lesson. And, who knows what lies ahead for you? Regardless of how far you go in your pilot education with or without a co-pilot, I know this: at least one unexpected conversation will occur because you had the guts to get started.

CHAPTER SIX

What can I do, once I'm a pilot?

HOPEFULLY ONE DAY YOU'LL COMPLETE the required amount of hours, take that final check ride, and become a pilot. But then what? If you are planning a professional career either in the military or the civilian world, this roadmap will naturally be clearer. But if you're intention is to fly recreationally this chapter is to show some of the million opportunities available for you as a pilot. You've gotten this incredible skillset that you alone have worked hard all those hours to accomplish. Now it's time to take advantage of what the world has to offer. It's time to fill the pages of your nearly empty logbook!

If you're like me, one of the things that might have driven you to open this book is a desire for adventure. Once you have your license you can take an aircraft up whenever you want, and wherever you want. But what aircraft do you go flying in? So what do you do after your lessons are over?

Though the most obvious option that comes to mind for new pilots is owning your own plane, there are many other ways of flying on your own. The world of aviation is similar to your experience with cars. Some own their own, some rent, and then there are the alternatives in between. There are many options available and the best alternative is the one that fits your needs and lifestyle. Let's go over the four most common ways:

Rental

One common avenue for new pilots is to rent an aircraft at the local aircraft rental places. You'll be quoted a "wet price", which means that the price you get per hour is included a full tank of fuel. As soon as the engine starts, the dollars start flowing. In some cases, if you are new to the rental company, they might go up in the air with you for a short trip to see that you are qualified to take their plane away alone. You got to wonder how sales would drastically decrease for Hertz and Avis if this was a common practice when it came to car rentals.

A note on rental aircraft (your trainer helicopter and airplanes included): Don't be surprised that the airplane doesn't match your expectations considering the hourly cost. These machines are usually old and beat up. But there is a difference between old and broken. The maintenance of aircraft is a lot more frequent than with cars and will therefore often run perfectly fine longer

However, if you see something, make sure to investigate. I heard of horror stories where rental places would try to pass aircraft as brand new with a fresh coat of paint. Even though you're new to airplanes and helicopters, listen to your gut. If you are unsure how to approach the topic, one flight instructor I spoke to, suggested asking to look over the maintenance records of the aircraft you're renting. If there are any terms you don't understand, you can always ask another pilot or look it up online. This will give you a general overview of performance and any recent issues, and more importantly if those have been fixed or not.

A common phrase in aviation is "trust, but verify". Through your lessons, you'll get used to following a pre-flight checklist to inspect the aircraft. Even when you're just starting out, keep in mind that at some point you'll be doing pre-flight checklists without any assistance, so the sooner you are able to trust your instincts the better. Double-check and spend the extra time. Many accidents could've been avoided if the pilots had the confidence to trust their instincts.

Shared ownership

Another approach to flying without buying a plane outright on your own is shared ownership with a group. This also has another fancy term that's commonly used, equity ownership. Equity ownership happens when a group of pilots come together to form a club and share the cost and ownership of an aircraft or multiple. You can choose to join spending cash or obtain a loan, it's all the same. The benefit is you get to spend less, but you'll have to share time in the cockpit and potentially other rules of the club. It's not to shove under a rug that humans are humans. Conflicts do happen, and sometimes it can be a little awkward in deciding how to proceed after someone doesn't want to be in the club anymore.

Non-equity group

Another format that's common is a non-equity group. You might have guessed it, this is the opposite of equity group, meaning you don't have any ownership in the aircraft. Confused? Don't be. It just means that instead of sharing ownership in an aircraft, a group of pilots share a lease of an aircraft or several. A benefit of leasing, just like in the car market, is that you can find more affordable deals on newer aircraft. However, since it is a lease, you're at the mercy of the original owner of the aircraft. If the original owner, let's say

Mr. Boeing, wants his aircraft back, he might terminate the lease and you'll have nothing to your name.

For both equity and non-equity clubs, it's important to spend an extra minute reading the details of the arrangements. Don't read the paperwork like computer manuals that everyone tosses in the bin, but actually take the time to understand what you're committing to. There are too many stories of good people who didn't read the fine print and ended up with surprise bills from their clubs.

There are also different legal structures to look out for in terms of your legal and tax obligations. This isn't a legal book, so I'm just issuing you a friendly warning to consider engaging some experts to assist with those sorts of things when you get to that point.

Owning

Owning your own aircraft, fully or together with a partner, is certainly a possibility. The prices vary greatly, but for some, it might not be as unattainable as expected. There are some added costs that you have to factor into owning your aircraft, which include, but are not limited to, insurance, hangar space, and maintenance. If you're splitting the purchase with someone else, this might help alleviate some of the cost, but can possibly result in other forms of scheduling conflicts for the future. Keep in mind that though no one can stop you from buying a larger airplane with multiple engines, you will be stopped from flying it without the appropriate training and licenses.

With the amount of paperwork that goes into buying your own aircraft, you can safely compare it to buying a new house. Just like the real estate market, there is a sales agent who represents the seller, and sometimes a buyer agent (though not always). Once the deal has been made, an escrow is established, and there is even a pre-inspection scheduled. If you own your own house already or planning to in the future, you'll know that even though you know a thing or two before going into a transaction like this, this process can be lengthy and overwhelming.

Regardless of what option you should end up with, it's important to give thought to what you're looking for in your experience. Aviation brokers, the people that help buy and sell aircraft, suggest writing a list of what you are looking for. Not just in the type of aircraft, but also in what you'll be using it for. There are no embarrassing answers. Because you know what - you're the one who is going to fly the plane. Just as in previous chapters, dare to dream. Jackie Cochran's dream of being a traveling beauty sales rep turned her into a world record-breaking pilot and eventually advising the Space program.

Ok, so you now have access to an aircraft, what's next? As you embark on this journey, I can't recommend enough to reach out to pilots and hear their favorite flying stories. All my life I have loved going on road trips, but being able to travel while skipping traffic and flying over mountains is just a whole different ball game. Hearing pilot stories makes that feel even more attainable to the novice pilot. And you might be lucky to be brought along on an adventure. Here are some stories of what others have done with their licenses:

Mischa Irsch, a finance executive based in Boston, takes his two daughters to the beach in his airplane. From his local airport to Kayman by Martha's Vineyard, it takes only an hour and a half of flying to be situated on the beach, the two-minute walk from the landing strip the sand included. "It's a great family activity. We pack a cooler, some beach toys, and chairs, and it becomes a whole day adventure." Though initially the young girls were a little intimidated by flying, his

8-year-old daughter now thrives in the front seat and sometimes assists in talking to the radios.

Tony Kennedy, Vice President at Xerox, also uses his flying as a way to inspire his daughters. He shares "when my daughter Aria asked me if she could go to space, my wife and I came up with the idea to take her up for a night flight to see the stars. I am not an astronaut, but I am fortunate to have my private pilot's license and have flown for the past 24 years. She was thrilled during the flight and got a chance to see the stars and fly over our house."

Greg Brown writes about both his national and international adventures in his airplane, named the Flying Carpet. One of my favorite stories is when Brown and his wife bring their Canadian friends on a flying trip to the small communities of New Mexico, called Grant and Milan, to explore a 1,000-year-old mud-brick city. Or less on the adventurous side, but more on solving the ancient how-can-I-be-two-places-almost-at-the-same-time-problem, Brown makes it happen more than once by offering to fly people to make it happen! You can read more of his stories in his book and the AOPA online column named after his airplane.

Professional photographer, Filip Wolak, and art director turned pilot, Sarah Tamar Kohan, combined their talents into a project called Flamping Across USA. When the world shut down in 2020 due to the pandemic, they found themselves with plenty of time to fill. Both loving flying and camping coined a new phrase "Flamping". The two documented the journey across the country on their blog inspiring others to learn how to fly and experience the freedom it gives.

CEO and Director of Los Angeles of Contemporary Art, Michael Govan, is someone who has flown all over the country since he got his license in 1995. Yearly he flies to visit museums in smaller towns all over the US as well as visiting some of the art projects he's personally involved in, such as

James Turrell's Roden Crater and Michael Heizer's City. He also discovered what was to become the venue for the Dia:Beacon while flying over the Hudson River. "I've had so many great flying experiences, but one of my favorite trips is the one I nicknamed "From the Hollywood Sign to the Statue of Liberty" with my daughter", he told me. Prior to the trip, his daughter had learned some basic flying so this was the perfect opportunity for her to hone those skills. "Even though we'd spent 21 hours in the air together, there had been no blowouts. In fact, we were attuned to each other as we had never been before. Our moods and even our music preferences were aligned."

Dr. Ing. Gerd Berchtold, an aviation consultant and former CEO of Diamond Aircraft, told me that from the first experience of flying he was hooked. "Flying is like a virus, and I've been infected a long time." As a part of his negotiations to work for Diamond Aircraft, he personally flew one of the company-manufactured airplanes from his home in Germany to the headquarters in Austria every week. In addition to some amazing flying experiences, he was able to identify many key improvements in the cockpit. Though based in Europe, he also has had incredible trips in the U.S., including watching the sunrise in Monument Valley and Bryce Canyon, flying into Death Valley, and seeing grizzly bears on the runway in Alaska. "Nothing beats seeing the world from above" he explains.

So what about international trips? Going international requires a little bit more planning, but is definitely not out of reach. The great thing is that the international language of aviation is English. In some places, you might encounter some resistance to speaking English on the radio, but regardless you'll most likely come out with a great story to share with your friends and family. In addition to planning your route and fuel, there might be some additional paperwork involved in crossing borders. But from the stories I've heard, it's all worth it.

Miles O'Brien wanted to be a pilot for as long as he can remember. His dad let him sit in the right seat from an early age and he got his private pilot license as soon as he was able to. As a long time jourrnalist and correspondent for CNN and PBS, he has many incredible flights in his logbook done for both work and pleasure. But when asked about which one was his favorite flight experience, he fondly spoke about a family trip that happened many years ago. He and his family flew a smaller plane from island to island in the Caribbean.

Another pilot who started flying at a young age and had numerous international trips under his belt was Bruce Rose. He holds an airline pilot license and type ratings for a few larger planes. Rose told me about some of his favorite trips to Europe with his wife. One time they flew from Long Beach to Croatia through the top of Maine to Gandor, through Reykjavik before they continued on to Europe in his Global Express. The Global Express is a larger jet airplane that requires not only Rose's qualifications, but an additional pilot to operate. He shared many other great travel stories but said they all have one thing in common - a long flight is only successful to him if his wife Rosemary has been comfortable.

Some might argue that traveling long distances on a Global Express or airplane of that size is both more comfortable and faster. But with some effort, you can go around the world in a smaller airplane. Julie Zang was 39 years old when she decided to leave her advertising career in China for the U.S. to become a pilot. Not long after did she embark on the ultimate international flight when she became the first Chinese and the eighth woman in history to circumvent the world. She did so in 18 days after 155 hours and flying over or landing in 28 different countries. Now that's an adventure!

Another way to find new avenues for your flying is to join a volunteer organization. You can practice your skill while doing good. There are so many wonderful opportunities to volunteer that come with an airplane or helicopter license. Including helping people who don't have the means to travel get to a hospital, transporting rescue puppies, or even showing the wonderful freedom of flying to someone who hasn't flown before. Some of the most accomplished pilots I spoke with have and continue to volunteer. It's a common misconception for new pilots that they can't afford to volunteer, but in reality, there are opportunities for any pilot who wants to be of service, regardless of whether you have the funds or not.

An additional benefit of joining a volunteer organization is that you get exposure to many different kinds of pilots. Long-time hobby pilot Gary Paquette volunteers with the Civil Air Patrol on a monthly basis fly with other hobby pilots, but also military and airline pilots. "We pick up different nuances from each other. The funny thing about professional pilots is that they are often working with a crew that prepares the aircraft for them. Though they might have more hours in the air, they learn from us hobby pilots and our extensive experience in doing our own preparations as well!" he explains. The Civil Air Patrol, according to their website, is there to search for and find the lost, provide comfort in times of disaster and work to keep the homeland safe.

One pilot I spoke to was inspired to start his own non-profit after having been involved with the Pilot for Day initiative at the military base he was stationed. "Being of service, in general, is good for everyone. A little bit of time and effort can have a life-changing effect for a child and their family," says Rob Balzano, founder of Check-6 Foundation. Check-6 mission is to provide aid, assistance, experiences, purpose, inspiration, and hope to children battling serious illnesses and military veterans in need. He's often asked if it's hard to continue doing what he's doing when so many of the children have passed. To that he answered "We can't change what the situation that they are going through, but we can try to replace some of those bad memories the families are left with after their son or daughter with some good memories." He often hears from the families years later that they still remember that day when their kid got to forget about their illness for a minute and be the pilot of an airplane.

There are many opportunities online, here is a list of the ones I came across in my interviews:

- Adopt a Pilot
- Angel Flight
- Challenge Air
- Legacy Flight Academy
- My Dog is my Copilot
- Pilot n Paws
- Pilot for Patients
- The Ninety-Nines
- Veterans Airlift Command
- Young Eagles

But can fly for an airline once you get your license?
Hold on there cowboy, not so fast. When you have your private license and instrument rating you still can't fly for money. In other words, if you're taking your friends flying you are not allowed to charge them for putting in the long hours or even for the rental or fuel. To be able to do so you'll need a commercial pilot license. In addition to additional education, you'll need 250 hours of flying before you can obtain your commercial pilot license. With the commercial license in your pocket, you can start charging dollars for your time in the air, but still under certain conditions.

In order to become an airline pilot on commercial flights, you will need to upgrade your commercial pilot license to an airline transport pilot license, ATP. Personally, I confused the term commercial license with how we use the word commercial pilot. A commercial license allows you to charge a fee, but most of us refer to airline pilots as commercial pilots. Rules changed in 2011 to require 1,500 hours of flying to be able to qualify for the ATP. FAA states "Unless otherwise exempt, you must have 1,500 hours before applying for an ATP certificate, including 500 hours of cross-country time, 100 hours of night time, 50 hours in the class of airplane for the rating, 75 hours of instrument time, and 250 hours of time as pilot in command." The FAA reduced this requirement for military aviators and for pilots who've gotten a pilot degree at an accredited college.

Many pilots, therefore, get paid for jobs that they can qualify for under the commercial license in order to get to the required hours of an airline transport pilot license. These jobs include parachute flying, banner towing, emergency and rescue, aerial photography, border patrol, coastal surveillance, law enforcement, agricultural and crop-duster. Once an aspiring pilot has flown commercially, at least 250 hours, they can get qualified to become a flight instructor.

To fly for an airline, you will also need additional training and certifications for what kind of aircraft you'll be flying on the job, aka type ratings. There is a big difference between a single-engine Cessna (the most common starter airplane) and a Boeing commercial jet you typically travel with. These ratings are usually a minimum amount of hours logged in that specific aircraft followed by a final check ride. After getting the required licenses, pilots often progress to a regional airline, such as Delta's Endeavor Air, or a transportation company, such as FedEx, before applying for one of the major airlines.

Even with all that training and experience, you also want to make sure your application sticks out from the candidates. The majority of airlines will expect you to have a Bachelor's degree at the minimum. And most job listings will have their own desired amount of hours in the air, education, specific languages, plus. "You spend a lot of hours as a team of two in the cockpit. Airlines like seeing that you have experiences outside aviation. Volunteering especially is a plus on your resume" explains Jessica Wolcott, a Detroit-based pilot who works for one of the largest airlines in the world. It can get boring if the other person doesn't know to engage in a conversation beyond aviation.

The airlines are looking for great team players, but also those who are able to speak up in case of an emergency. Every year the airline industry invests millions of dollars in crew resource management (CRM) and multi-crew coordination training (MCC) to improve the communication onboard. "One of the biggest risks in-flight accidents is that the communication between the two pilots isn't strong" explained Florian Masserer over a video call from his vacation in Barcelona. His employer, RWL German Flight Academy GmbH, is one the largest flight academies in Europe, and every year helps airlines with both technical and interpersonal skills. In some cultures, there is a stronger trend of hierarchy in the cockpit, which can get dangerous if the co-pilot doesn't feel like he or she can speak up. Masserer shared a story about an airline that was blacklisted in Europe due to failing communication but was then able to break down its hierarchical patterns through hours of communications training.

One cannot write about airline pilots without mentioning that being a pilot does come with some professional and personal challenges. Although it has become significantly much safer to be a pilot, pilots more often have to fight to have a spot in the cockpit. Few industries have experienced such rollercoasters in hiring, such as hiring freezes and massive layoffs, based on world events as the aviation industry. There are large, more obvious events, such as post 9/11 and the COVID-19 pandemic, but there are also other situations that have caused massive furloughs in the industry.

On the personal side, it's no secret that the pilot lifestyle isn't for everyone. Many have to work routes from airports that are far from their home, which includes a lot of additional commuting. Depending on how long you have worked for your company, you might be assigned your schedule last minute. Being a pilot often means missing out on big events, such as family birthdays and weddings, due to work. Sure sometimes you'll be able to switch your schedule, but with a constant chase for seniority, you might realize that a short time sacrifice has to be made for a long-term goal.

The irony is that the aviation industry is consistently experiencing a looming pilot shortage. There are a few reasons for this. Historically most pilots came from the military, but there are not as many pilots as there used to be partly because of the increased use of drones and unmanned aircraft. Another major deterrent is the extensive training and the substantial number of service hours required to get hired by the airlines.

CEO at United Airlines, Scott Kirby, wrote recently "At United, we're convinced that the root of the problem is that it costs over $100,000 and takes five or more years to obtain all the training to become eligible to fly for a major airline." He's not wrong. Far too many pilots will quit before earning the right license. With no guarantees of employment and almost guarantee of a few furloughs, once you do get employed, you must really have the eye on the prize.

Another cause of the pilot shortage is that by FAA regulations pilots have to retire at age 65. Some predict that this means that half of the pilots who are in the workforce today will have to retire in the next 15 years. Estimates show that by as early as 2025, there will be between 34,000 and 50,000 fewer pilots than airlines need worldwide. If you dream of becoming an airline pilot, these numbers underline that there will be a need for you in the near future.

Want to fly for fun?
But what if you're not sure being an airline pilot is for you or maybe you just want to fly for fun? You can always decide along the way. There are plenty of stories of people who made their own paths.

Jack Kilkeary comes from a long line of pilots. His dad, uncle, and grandfather are all pilots and have run a charter and management company, L.J. Aviation, for more than three decades. Despite that, he wasn't convinced he wanted to join the family business and decided to go to college. Upon graduating with a business degree, he decided to go to flight school but was still unsure if flying professionally was for him. At some point during his training, he fell in love with flying. Fast forward to today he loves flying all over the country and working alongside his family.

When Lee Abrams was deciding to approach a career in aviation or media and music, he decided that if he was successful in the ladder he would be able to buy his own plane and fly whenever he wanted. He ended up building a very successful career, including co-founding XM Satellite Radio. He still brings that discipline and focus from media and music into the cockpit. "Every flight still has a sense of exhilaration," he explained when reflecting on why he continues to fly after more than 9,000 hours in the air.

Magnar Nordal spent seven years literally working in the

dark at a photo lab. During that time he had been an avid hang-glider pilot, he decided to pursue a career as a flight instructor. After a few years teaching in his home country, he was offered a job in France teaching commercial airliners, which initiated a journey of opportunities all over the world, including living in the Maldives where he spent his free time scuba diving. Today he lives in Thailand while working for an airline in Nigeria, shares his passion for aviation on his YouTube channel, and is a reminder of how big and small the world really is.

Even if you know you want to fly professionally, there is a whole world of opportunities beyond the airlines that are often overlooked. In addition, there are many other opportunities in general aviation. General aviation is a pilot term used to explain the type of flying that happens outside the military and airline industry. Many will argue that those jobs are on par or even better than flying for major airlines. Jamie Beckett, AOPA You Can Fly Ambassador, grew up with his dad being a Pan Am airline pilot. Though he followed in his footsteps and went to flight school, he chose a different path that suited his lifestyle better. Beckett and the You Can Fly team is hard at work to reverse the pilot shortage. "I am lucky to have a company car that happens to be an airplane. I can fly for work on a daily basis, but at the same time, be home for dinner with my family". He is a believer that everyone can become a pilot, whether you want to do it for work or for leisure. Other highly sought-after jobs include flying for transportation companies, such as FedEx, and flying corporate jets for private individuals and corporations.

You also might find other jobs in aviation outside the cockpit that fit you better. Michael Wildes was studying at Embry-Riddle to become an airline pilot only to discover that he enjoyed the business side of aviation better. He is now an accomplished journalist and podcaster in the industry while still continuing to fly for his own enjoyment. In other words, you don't have to burden yourself with having it all figured out from the gecko. Or as author, Franz Kafka, once said: "Paths are made by walking".

Learn to enjoy the moment

While I was writing this book I came across a LinkedIn post written by the UK-based pilot, Mark Blois-Brooke, who so beautifully summarizes how so many experiences their pilot journey:

The young instructor is on his twentieth circuit with the student in a Piper Cub at the little grass strip. Glancing up, he sees a Cessna 402 flying over at 5000ft. "Ah", he thinks "if only I had his job, life would be great!" The pilot in the old 402 is tired, it's turbulent and this is his fifth-day carrying parcels for a courier company. Overhead, he sees an airliner at 35,000ft leaving pure white contrails against the blue sky. "Ah", he sighs "What I would do to swap with him, flying at 500mph above the weather and going somewhere exotic!" The Boeing pilot is heading east into the evening sky. It's a long flight and at the destination, he will be on minimum rest. A bright object catches his eye above him, moving quickly. "That must the Space Shuttle", he thinks. "Wow, I'd love to swap places with him, what a machine!" The Space Shuttle commander, hurtling around the Earth at 17,000mph is looking out of the window with a powerful telescope. He spots the guy in the Cub doing his circuits at the grass strip. He nudges his co-pilot. "Hey, Bud, take a look. Do you remember those days? Life was great, wasn't it? Just flying around the patch with not a care in the world. Gee, I really miss that!" If there are two things that pilots excel at its nostalgia and the belief that bigger and faster is better. It's not always the case, learn to enjoy the moment.

Flying is a perishable skill. The FAA recognizes this and for that reason, you do have to keep your license current. Keep in mind you never lose your license necessarily, but you do have to fly ever so often to keep current. The requirement says that every two years you have to do a check ride with an instructor to ensure you are a safe pilot. If you decide to get a new license or rating within those two years, you get to skip the currency check ride. If you haven't flown in a few months, you won't necessarily have to do a check ride, but you might have to get some flight time in.

I have spoken to many pilots with several thousand hours in the cockpit and who, for some reason or another, were forced to take a break from flying. Not one of them said they didn't feel a little unsteady getting back into the cockpit. One retired pilot I spoke to who hadn't flown in two years said he would want at least fifteen hours with an instructor before feeling in control again. Despite having spent more than 10,000 hours in the air previously.

Most pilots don't recommend going more than a few weeks between each flight. But occasionally longer breaks will happen due to weather or personal conflicts, and some refresher lessons might be a good idea. Test pilot, Eskil Amdal, was forced to take a break after the plane he flew crashed due to an engine failure and he ended up breaking his back. When he started flying again after a few months, he gave himself extra time to get familiar with flying again. He would spend extra time on the ground to go over everything. But still had to bring up others in the cockpit for the first few flights, before he eventually found his independence again.

Unfortunately, a lot of people stop flying after big breaks because they're too embarrassed to ask for some extra flight lessons. Others I spoke to found it too intimidating to get back into the cockpit after a long break. However, the most successful pilots I spoke to didn't compare themselves with other pilots, rather yesterday's version of themselves. They saw the opportunity in those situations to become an even better pilot.

According to Rusty Pilots, a division of The Aircraft Owners and Pilots Association (AOPA), there were about half a million pilots in the U.S. alone that have taken a breather from flying during the pandemic. If you go to AOPA's website you can enroll in free webinars and online courses that cover some of the basics that are needed to get refreshed. Or get started (hint, hint).

With flying being such a perishable skill, it is important to find new challenges and fun activities that bring you up in the air and maintain your confidence in the cockpit. One of the best parts of flying is that you're in charge. Not only at the controls, but also how far or not, you want to go. Many decide to continue flying with their private license and no further training, while others decide to go after all sorts of ratings and licenses. It really doesn't matter what others do, because you are the pilot, both in the cockpit and of your own life.

CHAPTER SEVEN

A very brief lesson in aviation history

I HAVE TO ADMIT BEFORE starting this project I didn't find aviation history that interesting. But that's because I didn't know where to start my learning. Aviation history is so vast that it's impossible to cover in a chapter, and as much as I want to cover all the major milestones, it's impossible. August Post wrote in *The Curtiss Aviation book* originally published in 1912 "The history of aviation is very brief, expressed in years. In effort, it covers centuries." That was less than a decade after the first official recorded flight. That's now close to 120 years ago.

Learning some history is a great way of finding your own standing in the world of flying. It's a world that loves a good homage to a hero, the inventor of a certain concept, or a prior aircraft. Which personally I find kind of awesome. Why not pay tribute to people or places that have made an impact and honor history in that way? Also learning the story behind the meaning sometimes makes it easier to remember.

Today, we're surrounded by great options to help us get from A to B. And now we dreamingly joke about teleportation as the ultimate transportation. However, if we go back to the early days of this planet, for many people that ultimate dream was flying. We have to imagine a day where rather than being frustrated over the inefficiency of traffic-congested roads or being frustrated with long TSA lines to get to your gate, you only had your own two feet or the borrowed four feet of animal transportation.

The inventors in this space were visionaries but often had to wait years for recognition of their big dreams. If they were even so lucky to have something deemed a success. Often these brave inventors had to suffer years of being criticized and ridiculed. It's been said that though there were incredible efforts before the first flight was successful, most of the experiments were more assisted falls, instead of successful flights.

Dreams of flying have been around since the beginning of time, but let's start in the 1400s. Before the Hollywood *Da Vinci Code* blockbuster, the original code Leonardo da Vinci was trying to crack was how to fly. Being one of the first in the world to have access to paper, da Vinci used the space beautifully. It's clear from his drawings that he admired birds and their ability to fly. You've probably seen his early drawings of a man with wings and some pretty intricate flying machines. The designs never left the paper and were a well-kept secret for over 400 years.

About two hundred years later a French locksmith named Besnier decided to take it one step further and created his own wings and managed to glide small distances. Though he was able to use the wings to "fly", it also demonstrated that the hardest part of flying, isn't flying. Inventors through time kept thinking the key to flying was the takeoff when in reality taking off is a very small part of the process. Rather the biggest challenge to overcome was staying in the air and eventually landing.

Fast forward a few hundred years and one of the French Montgolfier brothers, Joseph-Michel, was watching wet laundry dry over the fire one day, which sparked an idea for him. Seeing that there were small pockets forming upwards when the clothing was drying over the flames, gave him the idea to create what became the first hot air balloon. His need to get up in the air wasn't a new idea for Joseph, he had already non-successfully tried jumping from the family house with his own made parachute. Successful parachutes weren't to be invented until many years later.

First using a paper bag to create a balloon, Joseph realized that if he could contain a higher volume of lighter gas in the balloon than the air around it, the balloon would lift into the air. By creating a bigger balloon containing even more hot air, he realized more weight would be able to take off from the ground. You'll often find that hot air balloons for that reason are called lighter-than-air aircraft.

Failing to make the balloon on his own, he recruited his brother, Jacques-Étienne, by writing him a letter saying: "..Get in a supply of taffeta and of cordage, quickly, and you will see one of the most astonishing sights in the world." In 1782, the Montgolfier brothers successfully launched an air balloon that floated for a couple of miles. The brothers continued to work on their inventions for the rest of their lives and would have public demonstrations that impressed audiences all over France.

After the Montgolfier brothers invented the hot air balloon, others were inspired and started dreaming of improvements. However, it wasn't until the 1880s that the French Army invented a balloon that could be controlled, meaning it could take off and land in the same location. Until that point balloons had relied on air currents to move around. Other than being used for observation of enemy terrain these balloons had no other real military advantage.

A few years later the most notable airship, the Zeppelin, named after its inventor, Count Ferdinand von Zeppelin, was invented. The nobleman had joined the military at a young age and over the years built his identity around his status as a commander in the Army. In his fifties, he found himself ostracized by the Army for an internal disagreement, which crushed him not only professionally, but even more so personally. At age 54, he became determined to regain his standing in the military and was set on creating a war-winning weapon. Not only did he dream of an airship that could be steered, but that would also have a rigid structure and that could drop bombs.

Though successful in flying three and a half miles with a 400 feet ship, which was by far the largest vehicle to be in the air at that time, the German military wasn't impressed. Many of us would've called it a day at this point, but Zeppelin refused to give up. Zeppelin had exhausted the capital he had raised and been given no accolades for this impressive build. Not giving up, five years later the Count built 2.0, though successfully faster in the air, the ship was sadly destroyed by massive winds shortly after landing.

At this point, Zeppelin, almost admitted defeat, but fueled by the advances of the French military, decided to double down on his efforts. He launched a national press campaign to announce his vision. Though he won the hearts of the German people, the military still thought of him as a laughing stock. Despite his airship being faster and airborne for 12 hours in comparison to the measly 15 minutes that the European rivals could show for, the military refused to put in an order for his ships. The German military required a 24-hour flight and 700 kilometers distance traveled before they would be impressed. Thousands of Germans were out in the streets to support Zeppelin in this test flight that turned out to be yet another disaster that ended up with the airship being burned down in a storm.

This time around, having the support of the people, what

happened was something that of a fairy tale. People from all walks of life started sending money to the inventor to keep his company afloat, a total of six million marks. Zeppelin went from being a target of ridicule for close to thirty years to the most popular person in Germany in his 70s. The Kaiser traveled to see him personally to award him the country's highest medal of honor and to finally place an order for one of his ships.

Going back a few years in history again, the builders behind the first powered heavier-than-air flight also experienced difficulties in convincing the military to purchase their inventions. Airplanes, as we know them today, use heavier than air principles meaning that lift is created by the flow of air over an airfoil. This concept had been used successfully in flights without power in gliders and kites many years before airplanes were invented.

This first powered heavier-than-air flight, however, accepted by most aviation historians, was successfully completed by the Wright brothers at Kitty Hawk in late December of 1903. Despite having invited people to come to witness their attempt that late December day, the brothers flew four times without any audience. A few weeks prior to the brothers' success, Samuel P. Langley had experienced a rather public humiliation with his failed attempt.

Langley with government funding had built the Aerodrome that unsuccessfully launched from a boat and crash-landed in the Potomac River. As a result, most media outlets were tired of writing about aviation and people in the streets didn't believe anyone would ever be successful. Though the invention was written about in the papers, the business was far from booming. Yet the brothers decided to dismantle their invention in fear of their idea being stolen. The brothers continued to tinker and worked hard to convince the military to buy their plane. Tragically the first person to die in an airplane crash, Lt. Thomas Selfridge during one of many demonstrations for the U.S. Army. Selfridge had been aviation's biggest supporter from the military.

However, when the war broke loose a few years after, the brothers got an order for their planes and they were back in business. The First World War was the first time airplanes were used in warfare, though mostly only for surveying land and situations. Commercial airlines and wars had a complex relationship from the very beginning. Inventors built and tested their planes in those beginning days. There was no separation between the builder and the pilot. It was a far cry from being a means of transportation. It was a far cry from the commercial airliners we've come to appreciate today. Cars and trains were considered faster, safer, more comfortable, and cheaper. Unless it was for the adrenaline rush, no one saw flight as a means of transportation.

The first commercial passenger flight took place in St Petersburg, Florida on January 1, 1914. Though it was a rather short flight, it saved the passengers from a 12-hour drive to circle the waters, since there were no roads that connected Tampa Bay at that time. Unfortunately, only after a few weeks in business, the airline discovered that flight transportation was not attractive to most, and with too much overhead the line closed. Across the Atlantic, the Zeppelins carried over 10,000 passengers, before also their commercial trips came to a halt due to World War I. The buy-in for commercial transportation wasn't there.

War became a necessary evil for air travel to see the light of day. World War I sparked the production of airplanes. The time between the first flight by the Wright brothers to First World War was short, and it soon became a race between countries and allies to have the biggest, fastest, most aggressive, and flexible airplanes. Despite being the country of invention, the U.S., had to rely on overseas production of airplanes, and by the time production was at the rate it had to be, the war was over. Now the military forces had airplanes and pilots, but no particular use of either. No one really believed another war would happen, so instead of continuing production and training, the surplus of airplanes were sold off. Most of the buyers were either sportsmen or daredevils, people who saw an opportunity, often referred to as barnstormers.

Barnstormers is a term for pilots who would travel around the country setting up flight circuses, making air stunts, and occasionally offering paid rides. Many historic pilot figures were either barnstormers or inspired to become a pilot because of one. Around this time was also when pilots were competing regularly to set world records. In 1924, the first flight around the world was completed by a team of U.S. Army pilots, the trip took 175 days. Charles Lindbergh, originally a barnstormer, became the first pilot to cross the Atlantic Ocean in 1927. Amelia Earhart followed suit a year later to become the first female pilot to cross the pond. In the next few years, world records of speed, distance, and altitudes were set frequently.

It was only with money from the government to strengthen the military, that technology took place. The commercial side of aviation was second. 1926 is considered to be the first year of commercial airlines, before this really only cargo and mail had been carried by air for longer periods of time. But these airlines were far from glamorous these first few years. The cabins were cold, noisy, and smelled of fumes from the engine. Going from the West Coast to the East Coast by air would take close to 33 hours in travel, excluding the time spent changing aircraft on six to eight legs.

However, with many visionaries dreaming of a future of commercial travel, major development both in terms of distance and comfort resumed after the war. Two of the most influential visionaries were the founder of Pan Am, Juan T. Trippe, and Trans World Airlines owner, Howard Hughes. And in Europe, both KLM and Air France were founded and quickly became big players in the business of air transportation. Also, around the same time, laws were put in place forcing Boeing to separate its aircraft manufacturing operation from its airline business, which resulted in the formation of United Airlines. In just a few years airplanes were both more comfortable and faster. In February of 1934, Douglas DC-1, one of the earliest commercial aircraft that had room for 12 passengers set a new record. The DC-1 flew from California to New Jersey in just over 13 hours.

Unfortunately, another World War broke out and commercial aviation handed over their aircraft for military use. In the build-up to the Second World War, there was an incredible innovation when it came to aviation. Having been slow to react during the first war, the U.S. was determined to increase aircraft productivity in the 1940s. Running manufacturing plants 24/7, it is estimated that there were 300,000 American aircraft produced during the war.

Beyond increased speed, the airplanes got safer and larger and were equipped with many additional features, such as the possibility to use weapons and bombs. The secrecy behind new designs was crucial for the competitive advantage and sparked years of rapid innovation. The first helicopter was introduced by the Americans in 1939. The Japanese had developed the Zero in 1940, which was used to bomb Pearl Harbor the following year. The Germans then introduced the first fully jet-propelled engine airplane in 1941, which was ground-breaking technology. In 1945, the U.S. got their revenge on the Japanese by having the first plane capable of carrying an atomic bomb, Boeing B-29 Superfortress. This war set the stage for aircraft combat.

After the dust of the Second World War had settled, the major airlines faced an incredible boom in the 1950s, also often called the jet age. With the introduction of the jet engine, the focus of the aviation industry became the transportation of both cargo and passengers. The need for larger passenger airplanes initiated a competition between many manufacturers that eventually Boeing dominated. Simultaneously, Pan Am built an international business and sold 28 million tickets. The company become an object of status and the pinnacle of luxury and glamour.

In 1969 the first supersonic transport flight is a success and only a few years later Concorde started its operation of transporting passengers using this technology. The incredible technologic advancement meant that a trip from London to New York took only three hours. With enormous capital investment put down in research and development, legal bans from multiple countries to operate, and the unfortunate crash that left 100 passengers dead, the company was never financially profitable and ended operations in 2001.

Air travel for many decades after remained synonymous with Boeing, until Airbus was founded in 1970. The French manufacturer entered the market and aviation's biggest rivalry commenced. Some say it was this intense competition between the two that made Boeing make some disastrous choices in launching their 737 Max in 2018. In trying to compete with Airbus's A320neo, Boeing failed to disclose some pretty significant changes and undermined the need for additional training on those, which resulted in two tragic accidents, Lion Air Flight 610 and Ethiopian Airlines Flight 302.

Reading aviation history and its innovation is also beneficial for another reason. By learning about the development of technology and the determination of pilots, one can appreciate how far we have come and what bravery it took to get here. Realizing that when you step into that cockpit for the first time, you'll be doing with a safe flight instructor in an aircraft that has undergone massive maintenance requirements flying in an airspace that is controlled by a system of rules and regulations to ensure flight safety. Pilots before us didn't always have those benefits.

In addition to the enormous development created by designers and engineers that we've seen from the moment of the first flight, we have so much to thank the many brave men and women who took the risks in the cockpit. Many of them have been honored, some will always remain unknown. Fortunately, some stories have been uncovered and celebrated later, though some might say too little too late.

Some had to fight harder than we will ever imagine getting into the cockpit. Not because of financial reasons or geographical challenges, but because of who they were. An example is the Tuskegee Airmen, famously known as the Red Tails. Brave men that worked against discrimination for being of different skin color. They were some of the most incredible pilots during World War. Unfortunately, they didn't get celebrated as the heroes that they were when they returned back from the war. If anything some might say many tried to keep their bravery a secret. Fate had it that I met the son of one of the Tuskegee Airmen during my research for this book.

Ray Wilson, the son of Tuskegee Airmen Myron "Mike" Wilson, told me his father would avoid talking about what he did in the military. Whether he was humble or wanted to forget, Ray thought for most of his childhood that his dad was a chef in the military. His dad, always unable to sit still in front of the TV, didn't move while the two of them together watched the 1995 blockbuster *The Tuskegee Airmen* years later. "He recognized all the characters in the movie and was able to recount those stories," Wilson said. Today, rightly so, you can see many aircraft with a red tail or named after these legendary pilots.

There are so many more untold stories. But by learning some, you start connecting dots between what things are named or understanding why certain things were invented. Reading about a time when radios were not a part of flight safety, makes it easier to take pride in learning to overcome the fear of radios. Or instead of rushing through checklists and pre-flight inspection, you start noticing how certain parts are connected. And knowing the past, you can't help but admire todays and future dreamers and disruptors. Which begs the question, what does the future of aviation look like?

As I started writing this book, a few had asked me why I bothered, when the moment all pilots will be replaced by unmanned aircraft is just around the corner. Well, I'm not making the case that this isn't going to happen at some point. But all my research shows that at this point we don't exactly know where that technology is going or more importantly when we'll arrive there.

That being said as I'm writing this book, I'm excited about the many projects that are currently happening around the world. Unlike designs that are meant to be on Earth, designs that are meant to be airborne require more than simple, scalable engineering. And looking at how far we got from the early days of the Wright siblings in the early 1900s to today, there are most definitely exciting days ahead.

Some of the challenges that the aviation world is trying to combat are the use of fuel, congested airports, and noise levels, all the while preserving safety restrictions. One of the most prominent technologies that are being worked on in 2022, is the vertical take-off and landing, VTOL, technology for personal air vehicles. VTOL technology and the term started with the invention of the helicopter in 1907, but the development that is taking place these days is combining the flight experience of how an airplane lands with the taking-off capabilities of a helicopter. The dream of the future is for the freedom of consumers to take off from their own backyard, fly on their own through the skies, and park at their next destination.

In addition to building these hybrid airplane helicopters, there is a push to make these electric. This technology is called electric vertical take-off and landing, EVTOL. Some of the startups in this space are also promising to be autonomous. One expert in the space who has behind-the-scenes insight into this industry could inform me that a lot of the current projects have been able to get their funding by convincing sales pitches with the help of computer graphics. The real issue that needs to be solved before EVTOL can be a reality is the payload and battery equation. Simply put, in order for an aircraft can take-off powered by batteries there needs to be a huge development in the weight of the batteries. "You take off with the same weight as you land, unlike engines powered by fuel where the weight gets lighter over the flight time", he explained. Though this is an exciting part of our future, there are some real obstacles that need to be solved in order to get there.

Korum Ellis, founder of the Australian electronic aviation startup, Fly on E, is excited for the future, but keenly aware of the challenges ahead. "I believe it is only a matter of time before the technology can solve the diminishing return when it comes to battery and weight, but in the meantime, we are using a hybrid electronic aircraft in our flight training". The electronic airplane on the market today that Ellis uses has a 1-hour battery life and can hold only two passengers. Yet it is an exciting promise of the future: it is less noisy, cheaper to operate, and has less to zero-emission in comparison to traditional aircraft.

There are other exciting developments in aviation. There is a project headed by the founder of Worldwide Aeros, Igor Pasternak, focused on building the world's first cargo airship. The company has been working on the carbon-free carrier since 2010 and was set back by the pandemic and other development challenges. Other projects include flying cars, though not unfeasible to get off the ground, the biggest hurdle for these inventions to get through is legal. "One thing is getting a car approved for the road, another thing is getting the aircraft approved for the air, it's a whole different legal scenario getting the flying car approved for both", a source who was on the board for one of these projects told me. Skeptics say we're years from any major invention in this space, while others say we're in the third wave in aviation.

I wish I could share the many more stories and perspectives of all the advancements in aviation I covered in my research, but hope that this very brief lesson can make you look to aviation in even more wonder than before. Beyond the tangible aircraft developments we see in aviation history, there are the the incredible individual journeys. It's easier to appreciate elements of flying when you look at how far we've come. Loud cockpits due to noisy engines are nothing when you know look back and think of the first inventors risking all they had, to not only get in the air but hopefully prove their idea would work.

For decades after pilots risked their lives for innovation and to better this world. Personally, reading aviation history and pilot autobiographies has made me appreciate aviation so much more. Aviation history shows us how visionaries had to go against the logic of physics, tune out the naysayers and be rulebreakers to create the flying machines that changed the world.

CHAPTER EIGHT

What am I looking at?

WHEN READING ABOUT AVIATION, AN overwhelming part is the number of different aircraft there are. There are so many different names of helicopters and airplanes it is hard to keep them apart. According to the *Telegraph*, there are some that say there are close to 150,000 different aircraft in the world. Others say there are only 39,000 different kinds, but that's still a substantial number. Or how the legendary pilot, Ernest Gann, put it in his book *Fate is the Hunter*: "The only characteristic all airliners share is that upon proper urging they are normally capable of leaving the earth's surface. Otherwise, the various types, regardless of their natural origin, an individual as breeds as of animals." The amount of different aircraft that have been introduced after Gann wrote that in 1961, is not insignificant.

When I was doing research for this book, there were times I would ask the interviewee to repeat the name of the same plane or helicopter multiple times. Other times I would hurry to write down what I thought they had said so I could look it up later. It made me wonder if I was the only aspiring pilot who didn't know the names of aircraft. Then one day I had an epiphany. Aircraft are like cars.

I went to the legendary Lime Rock Park Historic Festival in Connecticut a few years ago. The festival hosts a car race that attracts hundreds of vintage cars and their owners. I had no idea what kind all the cars were. I would ask when I saw a car that made me curious, and other cars that didn't interest me, those I would blissfully ignore. Sure there were many people there who would be able to tell you the make, year, and further details to almost every car there, but it didn't bother them or me that that wasn't me. Whenever I had a question I would ask and it would spark interesting conversations. I will make the argument that some of them even enjoyed sharing their passion with a novice. A new audience that won't argue facts and details of the car, but is just interested in learning the basics. The same goes for pilots and helicopters and airplanes.

If you find yourself in a conversation about aircraft and don't know it, don't be scared to ask. Very likely you'll be giving someone an opportunity to talk about something they enjoy. And if you really want to learn about not only aviation history but different makes and models, seek an aviation museum. Or better yet if you get the chance go to OshKosh. The last week of July every year the small town Oshkosh in Wisconsin turns into a mecca for pilots and aviation aficionados as it hosts the world's largest airshow, EAA AirVenture Oshkosh. According to the festival's website, there were over six hundred thousand people in attendance with over 10,000 different types of aircraft in 2021. If you want to get a close view of many different types of aircraft through time, this is the place to be.

In the next few pages, I will attempt to dissect the history behind some of the naming conventions and give an overview of some of the most common kinds that you'll come across. For obvious reasons, I have it kept very high-level.

Just like the lack of standardization was seen in design and manufacturing in the beginning days of aviation, there is no solid common thread in the naming convention of aircraft. From the beginning, just like we've seen through history, designers and manufacturers wanted to put their names on their projects. Just like famous painters would initial their paintings in the corner, these individuals wanted to put their stamp on their work.

Beyond the name of the company, each manufacturer would use its own naming system. If you've ever been to the Swedish furniture store, IKEA, you'll find that each product has a name according to category. Dining tables and chairs are named after Finnish places, chairs and desks are male names. This was the system that the founder Ivar Kamprand put in place to quickly distinguish the items in his inventory. This personal spin is something that you recognize in the early days of aviation. Names were at first an afterthought, an easy way to distinguish. Glenn C. Curtiss explains in his book, *The Curtiss Aviation Book:* "Following our custom of giving each machine a name to distinguish it from the preceding one..."

Most manufacturers were working in isolation in those early days. There was a need to be the first, the fastest, the safest, the most efficient, but there was no desire to collaborate. It took ten years from the first flight to some form of standardization of the aircraft. This standard didn't apply to a naming convention, but there were some trends. The first aircraft were given simple names with credit spotlighting the designer. The first plane that the Wright Brothers introduced was named *Wright Flyer*, their second version *Wright Flyer II*. Around the same time across the Atlantic, the French aviator and inventor Louis Charles Joseph Blériot called his gliders and later airplanes Blériot I, Blériot II, and so on.

When a design was built by a larger group the design

would rather be named after something else to not give credit to one individual, but the group. One of the first aircraft to fly after the Wright Brother's success was the *June Bug*. Built by Glenn Curtiss for *Aerial Experiment Association* under the leadership of Alexander Graham Bell, also famously known for inventing the telephone. It's believed Bell gave this name because the plane was completed in June. When Curtiss later ventured out on his own, his first plane was called Curtiss No. 1.

Designers and engineers were working in isolation all over the world. But you can see this personal branding happening in other places than the U.S. as well. Legendary British aircraft designer, Sir Geoffrey de Havilland used his initials in the names of the aircraft while he worked for the manufacturer, Airco. The DH4 was a frequently used airplane during World War I and later at the beginning of the U.S. Postal Service by air. When he later founded his own company, he got more creative and would use descriptive words for his designs. De Havilland developed the Mosquito that some have claimed to be the most versatile airplane to ever have been built. Not unexpected with those kinds of accolades success, there were also unofficial nicknames given by the public. The Mosquito was called "The Wooden Wonder" or sometimes "Mossie" as well.

Because so much of the early development of airplanes took place during the wars, many of the traditions stem from this era. Often named after birds, descriptive names would often encompass function. Some examples of airplanes that were used for observation were given bird names such as Seagull and Kingfisher. On the other hand, aircraft with dive-bombing as their key function had names, such as Avenger, Devastator, and Dauntless. Often you will see as the airplane advanced, the name followed. The Boeing Flying Fortress became the Super Fortress. The Hellcat became the Wildcat.

Another situation that happens when companies work apart is that different planes will have the same name. And over time, manufacturers probably ran out of names and reused earlier ones. In 1974, British manufacturer group, Hawke Siddeley developed a trainer airplane for the Royal Air Force named Hawk, but the original Hawk was the Curtiss Hawk built in the 1920s. Curtiss used many versions of the Hawk name, mostly for fighter planes, including Skyhawk, Tomahawk, and Mohawk. The last one in the Curtiss series was called Kittyhawk, which is the field the Wright Brothers had their first landing. Despite the original conflict between Curtiss and the Wright brothers over patents, their two companies eventually merged to form Curtiss-Wright, which still operates today. Also, one of the most common beginner planes is called the Cessna 172 Skyhawk.

While military aircraft were often given predatory animal names, commercial transportation models were given names that alluded dreamy comfort of travel. Donald Douglas was just a kid when he watched the Wright Brothers demonstrate their invention to the U.S. Army. While others were satisfied with having witnessed an extraordinary performance, this moment changed Douglas's life. Douglas from that moment on had dreams of flying people around the world in larger airplanes. The first aircraft he designed under his own umbrella was called the Douglas Cloudster. He then went on to develop the World Cruiser which he sold to the Army and the Douglas Sleeper Transport that airlines bought for passenger transportation. When he further developed the Sleeper Transport, those were named Sky Lounges and Skysleeper.

Unbeknown to anyone, there seems to always be one part of a name that is the one that sticks. In the case of the most successful commercial airplane for most of history, the Boeing

737, became known as the 737. The naming convention at Boeing has not transpired linearly since being founded by William Boeing in Seattle in 1916. The first plane, the Boeing Model 1, was known as the *B&W Seaplane* after both the founder and the co-designers initial Conrad Westerfelt, a lieutenant in the U.S. Navy. After the world Boeing created the Boeing Model 6, also known as B-1D, where the B stands for Boeing to distinguish this aircraft wasn't intended for military experiments. Today a B in front of an aircraft signifies that it's a bomber, an aircraft that carries bombs.

Many of the helicopters and airplanes you still see today carry the name of their original inventor from the early days of aviation. Cessna, Piper, Beechcraft, Boeing, Lockheed Martin, Northrop Grumman, and McDonnell Douglas are among many companies that have survived through iterations from the early days. For companies that have themselves gone through massive transformations, it makes sense that there are so many different names and naming conventions.

It's OK to not know

All this to say, learn why aircraft are named what they are named, you learn a slice of history. Learn aviation history, and you're more likely to recognize why airplanes are called what they are called. Realize that you should never be ashamed to not know a model or type of aircraft someone is telling you about. There is so much history and innovation that it isn't possible to know them all. When I asked Roger Noble who has spent his entire career in all aspects of aviation about this, he said "over the years you learn by frequency and assimilations."

But like knowing every car type isn't a requirement for driving a car, knowing every type of aircraft does not make you a better pilot. I spoke to a long-time pilot who openly admitted that beyond the airplane he flies for work, he has no interest in other types and models. He'll politely speak airplanes at parties but secretly doesn't have much interest.

A lot of people are into flight and aviation.. that's cool and all, but I find the whole thing rather Boeing - **unknown**

If you find yourself in a conversation not knowing a model, just ask. Most of the time you'll find that people will want to explain more about the aircraft and probably want to show you pictures. Like any pilot will admit, pilots like to speak about flying and you might suddenly find yourself in a lot longer conversation than you were expecting. Now let's move onto some of the more common helicopters and airplanes you will hear about:

Trainer Aircraft

The two most common trainer airplanes in terms of numbers are Cessna 172 and Cirrus SR22. Both of these are used by the military for the preliminary 25-hour training for prospective flight school pilots. These are by looking at sales numbers over the last decades by far the most popular, but the school you end up going to might have other trainer planes. Some other common manufacturers to know of are Piper, Aviat, and Beechcraft. As of writing this book, Pipistrel Virus SW 121 is the only trainer-approved electric airplane in the world.

Cessna 172 Skyhawk was developed in 1956 by Cessna Aircraft Manufacturer, named after its founder Clyde Cessna. According to Cessna's website it "is the most popular single-engine aircraft ever built and has achieved a reputation for being the ultimate training aircraft."

Cirrus SR22 has been manufactured by Cirrus Aircraft since 2003. The SR22 is often referred to as the airplane with the parachute because of the safety mechanism that will be activated in emergencies.

Robinson R22 is the most common helicopter trainer. It has two seats and two blades, which makes it easy to remember 22. It was designed by Frank D. Robinson in 1979.

Military Aircraft

If you start your training in the military, each branch will have its own fleet of aircraft, but most military students start their training in a Cessna or Cirrus. Once military students have learned the basics of flying, or what in the civilian world equates to a private pilot's license, they move on to the military trainer planes. Military trainers are distinguished by the T in the name.

Once a military pilot is assigned his or her next aircraft, which is often referred to as airframe in the military, they move on to train in that one. Even if you end up being a helicopter pilot in the military, you have to learn how to fly an airplane first. Other military aircraft capabilities can also be distinguished by the letter, including A for Attack, B for Bomber, C for Cargo, F for Fighter, T for Tankers. Two of the most commonly used airplanes in military training are the T-34 and T-6A. These trainers are both manufactured by Beechcraft founded by William and Olive Ann Beech in 1932.

The T-34, full name Beechcraft T-34 Mentor, has one engine, two seats, and is propeller-driven. Some have been surprised how fast it can go, saying its looks are deceiving.

The T-6A, full name Beechcraft T-6A Texan II, also has one engine, two seats, and is propeller-driven. Similar models to the T-6 are used as trainer planes for by countries' military around the world, including Canada and Israel.

Commercial Airplanes

When it comes to commercial airplanes, the two most common ones are the Boeing 737 and the Airbus 320. Both of the airplanes were launched decades ago, but have been developed and modified over the years. One pilot I spoke to said the biggest difference of flying the two airplanes goes back to the philosophy of the two manufacturers. Boeing is described as an American workhorse while Airbus is a French engineer. "We often joke if something needs to be fixed on a Boeing a new procedure or checklist will be added, while if something goes wrong with an Airbus the software will be updated" he explained.

Boeing 737 was first introduced by Boeing in 1967. There are have been many variations of this airplane, and as of February 2022, there have been 15,000 737s ordered by airlines worldwide.

Airbus 320 was first manufactured by Airbus in 1984. There are many models of this airline jet that allows for transporting

between 107 to 230 passengers.

Now let's put some aircraft in perspective by comparing them:

Comparison of aircraft speed

9 mph	Hot air balloon
110 mph	Beginner helicopter
140 mph	Beginner airplane
850 mph	Commercial airplane

Speed

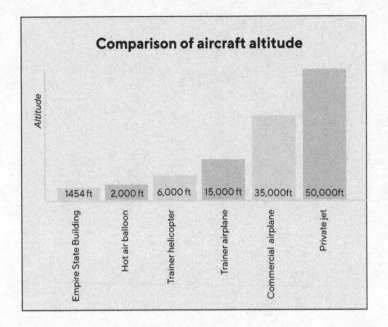

From this chapter, I hope you take away one thing: it is ok to not know what an aircraft model is. There are plenty of pilots who are terrible at telling manufacturers and models apart. One pilot I spoke to would count the windows of the airplanes to spot the difference between models of the same manufacturers. But just like you don't have to know all the car models in the world to be a good driver, you don't need to know all aircraft models to be a good pilot.

CHAPTER NINE

The questions you're too embarrassed to ask

BEING A NOVICE IN ANYTHING you'll be uncomfortable. You won't know everything. What are great questions, what are lame questions? Let me be the one to tell you, there are no lame questions. If someone makes fun of you for asking any question, they clearly have an issue. By the same token, I made a list of questions that I was too embarrassed to ask.

I use glasses/contacts, can I still fly?

You don't need a 20/20 vision to get your pilot license. If you were worried that you wouldn't be able to fly up in the skies because you have glasses, you no longer have to worry. As long as you have corrective lenses (contact lenses or glasses) and pass your medical the sky is literally the limit.

Don't fall into that category? You might still be able to embark on this journey. It's called a statement of disability ability (SODA) and is provided by further testing by SSFDO. One of the best pilots in history, Wiley Post, had only one eye. Post, amongst other achievements, is famous for being the first to solo the world. Please note that requirements might vary from country to country and also what kind of license you're applying for.

I am color blind, can I pursue my pilot license?

Color is an important part of aviation, and in the past any sign of color blindness automatically disqualified you, but it's not like that anymore. When it comes to color blindness, it depends on the severity of your condition. There is alternative testing that you should be able to discuss with your local flight school, so don't give up just yet!

Can I become a pilot if I have a physical disability?

"When someone with a physical disability ponders whether or not they can become a pilot, the general answer is an easy and encouraging one. For most people, the answer is yes, and that includes people who face significant mobility challenges," explains Charles Stites who founded Able Flight in 2006.

At an event in April of that year, a friend who imported and sold an Italian plane showed him a set of adapted hand controls that he said would be available in those airplanes later that year. Stites, who at the time was working as an aviation writer and photographer, suggested that once he had a plane with the controls it would be a story he would like to cover. A few weeks later he saw an article in a British magazine about a young woman who had lost the use of her legs in the 2005 bombings in London, and how a British scholarship organization was going to make it possible for her to learn to fly.

He began to look for a similar organization in the U.S. so that he could write about their story, and was discouraged to find there wasn't one. A few days later, he realized that all of the elements had come together to start a nonprofit scholarship organization here in the States, and he made the decision to completely change what he was doing in his career and decided to create Able Flight.

Within six months he had commitment of funds from a friend in the business. And with a generous offer to train the first two pilots by Jon Hansen, the gentleman who was importing the adapted planes, the organization granted their first two scholarships in December of 2006 and training began in 2007. The organization continues to annually support prospective pilots with physical disabilities with training and scholarships.

Stites adds, "Of course, there are individual circumstances that may make it harder for some than others. But with the availability of adapted aircraft for training, and with FAA medical certification requirements that created greater opportunities around 15 years ago, aviation has become far more accessible for more people."

What if I sometimes struggle with motion sickness?
One of the many reasons a demo flight is recommended is to see how you react to flying. Being in a smaller trainer aircraft is different than being a passenger onboard a commercial airline. Do you have a past of getting sick on boats or in cars? You might find yourself sick in the cockpit too. Airsickness is a form of motion sickness that can come creeping over your shoulder like an unwelcome surprise.

Discouraged? Don't be! Many pilots have experienced air sickness and gone on to have long pilot careers after. Chuck Yeager, the first pilot to break the sound barrier, struggled with air sickness but overcame it. Mike Van Wyk, a former pilot for the legendary air show demonstration team, U.S. Navy Blue Angels, told me he never overcame his air sickness. "I loved flying so much, but I knew being airsick would be an automatic disqualifier for flight school, so I hid it flight after flight."

Another pilot who struggled with air sickness was Kim "KC" Campbell. She started her pilot career at her local airport as a 16-year-old and didn't really feel the air sickness in the small trainer airplane she was training in. However, it was harder to ignore as it crept up when she got in faster and more complex airplanes in the military. "I would chair fly before every mission. Practice everything from start to finish, so when I got up in the air I knew what I was doing and could lean on my preparation when I got airsick." For Kim, her air sickness went away slowly over time and she went on to fly more than 2,200 hours in multiple U.S. Air Force aircraft in her career.

Looking for a way to combat air sickness? These are some ways to decrease the onset of airsickness:

- Don't eat too heavy of a meal before your flight lesson. Make sure you have something in your stomach but don't show up too full.
- Be hydrated
- Don't drink too much caffeine before getting into the cockpit
- Get a good night's sleep before your lesson. Lack of sleep can increase the risk of air sickness.
- A good workout can help your focus and also decrease the risk of air sickness
- Consider trying the Bárány chair

The history of the Bárány chair

Invented by Hungarian ontologist Róbert Bárány as a part of his research on the inner ear, the Bárány chair has helped many pilots cure motion sickness in the air. The person is blindfolded and seated in a spinning chair and the set of actions tricks the inner balance of the ear. If you go on YouTube, you can actually make a version of the chair in your own living room.

Is being a pilot a hobby or a profession?

Growing up I, and in my research, many others, believed the only way to become a pilot was to do it professionally. The truth is that there is no way of knowing what it will be for you before you're in it. You might have had the dream since you were 2 years old, and discovered you hate it. You might have just thought about it for the last two days, spontaneously gone up in a trial lesson, and loved it and now that's all you want to do. All day, every day.

In Cal Newport's bestselling book *So Good They Can't Ignore You*, he discusses that passion is sometimes found by coincidence. Like many people who end up loving what they do, he stumbled into his profession and then found that his passion for the work increased along with his expertise. You might love being in the cockpit, or you might have a conversation with someone at the airport that steers you in the complete opposite direction into the aviation world. Michael Wildes trained to become a professional pilot at Embry-Riddle only to discover he was more passionate about the aviation business side of things. Alexander Trent was studying economics in San Francisco when he asked a friend of a friend who was a flight instructor for one lesson, not long after he moved to Florida to become an airline pilot.

What is it like to work as a professional pilot?

If you do become a professional pilot, you'll have to be prepared for change. During my research, many pilots kindly asked me to forewarn my readers about the challenges of the profession. It is hard to land that first job, you'll be a new pilot with often fewer hours than others applying for that same position. Once you get the job, you'll be given the worst shifts, because the industry works on a seniority system.

And even when you build your seniority, you'll be working long hours and be spending many days away from your home. And it is historically a tough industry with many unexpected challenges. You don't have to look far back in time to see examples of massive turnovers. During the pandemic close to 50% of commercial pilots were laid off or furloughed. One pilot also wanted me to mention that you'll be completely fed up with baguettes. Or airport food in general.

Despite all of this, the majority of the pilots I spoke to would say with a big smile: it's the best job in the world.

How do I stay motivated on my pilot journey?

One of the ways is to tap into your inner motivation, "When I joined the Royal Air Force, I made a promise to myself that I was going to make it", Peter Docker told me reflecting over how he ended up becoming only two of fourteen pilots who graduated from his basic flight training group. Docker knows how crucial it is to connect to what is deeply important to us – what he calls our 'non-negotiables'. For many, these will include family, but will also include other non-negotiables that are revealed when we reflect on the choices we make in our lives. When we put these into words they become what we *stand for* and form part of our character.

Docker knows this from the pilot's perspective and also from his many years of research on the topic and practical experience leading others. Docker has brought his latest thinking together in his own book *Leading from the Jumpseat*. Docker passionately explained to me the reserve of energy that you can tap into if you know what you stand for – what really matters – and turn those stands into commitments. This applies to pilot training as much as it does navigating other aspects of our life. He writes in *Leading from the Jumpseat*, "This energy can propel us forward in the most challenging of times, helping us overcome the obstacles we meet. It can also sustain us when we fail along the way."

When is the best time to start to learn to fly?

The best time in life to start is when you feel ready to embark on an adventure. Flying is a hobby that requires time and money, but never forget if there is a will, there is a way. But you want to make sure you're not distracted by something outside the cockpit while you're in the air. You know your limits best, so don't let anyone be the judge of what you can put on your plate. But be honest with yourself. It is a lot more enjoyable if you can fully allow yourself to be in the skies without worrying about something else that is happening down on planet earth.

Most flight instructors recommend two to three lessons a week. There will most likely be rescheduling due to weather or other unforeseen events, and if you have only one lesson a week that can easily become two weeks between each lesson. Since flying is a perishable skill you want to avoid too big gaps in your learning so that you don't waste time and money having to relearn concepts.

Am I too young/old to become a pilot?

Legally one has to be 16 years old to solo and 17 years old to get your private pilot's license. Many would argue that even though you cannot legally fly before hitting your sweet sixteen, there are plenty of options to kickstart the learning. Pilots I spoke to who grew up with other pilots in their family or close surrounding family seemed to be a little less overwhelmed their first time in the cockpit. If you're a minor you can still get a headstart on your education. For instance, you can learn radio communication, go to the airport to create friendships, and watch videos on YouTube.

On the other side of the age spectrum, there is no maximum legal age. However, in order to get your private pilot's license, you will need a medical certificate from your doctor. Sometimes age-related medical issues can be a stopping factor in this case. If you're suspecting you might be in that category, it might be worth making sure you can get your medical certificate before investing too much time into your training at first. "You're never too old," said Florian Masserer, who works at a German flight school, "we just recently had someone in their 70s start working toward their private pilot license."

Am I too short? Am I too tall?

The height requirements didn't originate from vanity measures, but rather the level of operation. A pilot should be able to reach the rudder pedals while also being able to see out the windshield. But on the other side of the height spectrum, it can cause other issues. The famous author Roald Dahl who was a fighter pilot during World War II was 6'6" and had to cram himself into the cockpit and would sometimes suffer from intensely painful leg cramps.

There are no legal minimums or maximums when it comes to a pilot's height in the civilian world. Sometimes shorter pilots will need to get extenders to reach the rudder pedals, other times taller pilots will find that the lack of space will make it a little less comfortable in the cockpit. Historically, there were height requirements for professional and military pilots, but over time these requirements have loosened due to adjustable seats in modern aircraft. The U.S. Air Force still has height restrictions, but as of 2019 started offering height waivers to candidates that don't fall between the 5'4" and 6'5" requirements.

Do I have to be a neuroscientist to become a pilot?

The truth is that you don't have to be a genius to become a pilot. In my conversations, I was reminded over and over again that being a pilot doesn't require expert-level mathematics or super passion for science. More importantly, you'll need a determination to stay the course when the theory gets a little difficult. There were many I spoke to who admitted that the theoretical part of the training didn't come naturally to them, but with a good dose of determination, they were able to get through that part.

As a matter of fact, aviation legend Anthony Fokker, did terrible in school. The Dutchman behind the aircraft manufacturer company, Fokker, which still is around today, flunked regular schooling. He is not the only one. Aviation, past and present, are filled with examples of people who didn't do well in math and sciences or do well in traditional schooling, but became excellent pilots.

Is studying for the theoretical part of flying hard?

A lot of the pilots I spoke to talked about the importance of having an interest in flying and I couldn't help but think about the number of times I had opened the flying textbooks only to close them again seconds later. Though I've for the most part of my life actually enjoyed studying, flight training theory is challenging for me. Then I learned that many accomplished pilots have had the same problem and still do. In conversation with test pilot Eskil Amdal, who has flown over 120 different aircraft in his career, he admits it can still be challenging to grasp the theory. "Sometimes I have to read over and over again."

Flight instructor, Greg Brown, gives the following advice: "Don't start reading the books and manuals before you've been in the cockpit a few times". Part of the problem I faced, and what hundreds of pilots experienced before me, was understanding new concepts with a new language. Spending some time in the air and seeing things visually can help build some of the basic languages and see connections that are hard to get from a page in the book.

What happens if I fail my check ride?

Before you ever get into the cockpit, you should know that we all start from different starting points. Some aspiring pilots have grown up with flying in their family planes, others have obsessed over simulators as a pastime, others have no prior exposure. This is ok. No point in comparison. If you're less confident in the cockpit, remind yourself you most likely have other areas of expertise that your peers don't.

Now, what happens if you're having a hard time grasping the concepts? Or if you should fail your check ride? Nothing. You will not be punished or disqualified from trying again. Many very accomplished pilots have failed on their first chec -ride. And one pilot I spoke to even almost crashed on his.

U.S. Marine Corps helicopter pilot, Paige E. Rose, says " Just like sports, or actually most things in life, be willing to be really bad it. Take the losses and failures and make a conscious effort to make it right." UK-based pilot, Grace McKellar, echoed Rose in our conversations, "Pick yourself up again, some things are going to be really difficult. Make the decision that you need to finish." Despite the challenges, everyone seems to agree, the blood, sweat, and tears are worth it in the end for the sense of accomplishment waiting at the finish line.

I'm scared of flying, is being a pilot out of reach for me?

I was surprised in my research to realize that many pilots had originally been scared to fly on commercial airliners. One was an accomplished helicopter pilot, Albert Perez, who was afraid of flying before joining the U.S. Marine Corps. But after learning how to fly he realized it was an irrational fear. For some it was being in control of the aircraft themselves, for others it was learning more about how airplanes and weather conditions work.

Beware that fear of flying can appear for even already trained pilots. Take Mike T. for instance: "I became afraid of flying, in airlines as well, after having a tire blow on takeoff from Paris and having children. I overcame that fear by starting to fly myself again."

Keep in mind that most pilots believe it's healthy to not be completely fearless at any point in their flying career. There is a famous line often used in aviation: there are old pilots and bold pilots, but no old bold pilots. Red Bull pilot and test pilot, Eskil Amdal still gets a little nervous before every take-off and landing. "It's healthy to be slightly nervous, it's important for your overall performance."

What's the difference between aviator and pilot?

The words are used synonymously. Before the FAA was founded and no pilot license was required to fly (!) other than for performance shows, Aero Clubs around the world issued aviator licenses. The word "pilot" was originally used onboard ships. If you read the adventures of Ernest Shackleton or Fritjof Nansen you'll see pilots referred to often. And when the hot air balloon was invented, these were often named airships. Since ships had pilots, my guess is that eventually more people started using the word pilots. But all in all, they are the same.

Are there a lot of acronyms?

There are more than a lot of acronyms in aviation! In talking to experienced pilots, I was happily reminded that even they don't know them all. And that sometimes they will forget them still. Sometimes acronyms will mean different things for different industries. If you're a pilot in one of the military branches, you'll learn that the different branches use the same acronym for different things. And you might be coming from a different industry with a completely different set of acronyms. I would never make fun of anyone for asking me what a finance term meant in my day job. So if I don't know a term, I will just ask. Here are some common acronyms:

ATC	Air Traffic Control
ATIS	Automatic Terminal Information Service
ATPL	Airline transport pilot license
CPL	Commercial pilot license
CFI	Certified flight instructor
ETA	Estimated Time of Arrival
ETD	Estimated Time of Departure
FAA	Federal Aviation Administration
FBO	Fixed Base Operator (service provider at an airport)
IFR	Instrument Flight Rules
METAR	Meteorological Aerodome report (weather report)
PIC	Pilot in Command
POH	Pilot Operating Handbook
PPL	Private pilot license
VFR	Visual Flight Rules

Throughout your training, you'll also learn acronyms for certain maneuvers or actions during your flight. If you're not a fan of acronyms (looking at you non-American), you might as well learn to love them.

Where do I start?

You know by now that I am a big supporter of creating your own path. But here are stop steps do get you started:

1. Schedule an intro flight
2. Define your "why"
3. Choose your aircraft

4. Choose your pathway
5. Define the right instructor for you
6. Meet other pilots
7. Read aviation history
8. Stick to the path that you carve

If you choose the military or full-time pathway, they'll assign you your next steps. In order to get your private pilot license, you will need two things: a medical certificate and a student pilot license. Your third-class medical certificate is issued by an Aviation Medical Examiner (AME). The doctor visit will entail an eye test and some basic checkup elements to see that you're fit for flight. Though you don't technically need this for your student days, many pilots recommended getting this out of the way the sooner the better. If for some reason you, unfortunately, cannot fly this would be the ideal time to find out. Disappointing of course, but some might argue less disappointing than down the line. Even if you don't pass your medical, there might be ways of correcting the results.

Though you don't technically need a student pilot license before your first solo, some airports will require you to have one to get access to their landing strip. The process is fairly straightforward. All you have to do is submit the required paperwork to your school or directly to the FAA for processing. There is no direct fee with this card, but some schools might charge a fee to take care of the paperwork for you. Overwhelmed by the amount of effort and paperwork it requires to get started? Don't be. You don't need any paperwork for an intro flight. If you love it, the additional paperwork won't be an issue. Trust me.

As we part ways, you might be wondering where I am in my own pilot journey. Over the years, I wrote this book I spent most of my time studying aviation from the ground. I'm not aspiring to fly professionally, only as a hobby. And on my personal checklist for becoming a pilot is to learn in a way I enjoy and to have fun in the process.

My goal now that this book is in your hands is to find a high-intensity training program and complete my private pilot's license. I will spend a few weeks flying multiple hours a day. In those weeks, I intend to live and breathe flying and aviation! From other hobbies and skills I have honed over the years, I know this approach is the best one for me.

If you've learned something from reading this book, make sure to share it with others and help #demystiflying. You might inspire someone to go flying in the process! I hope that by reading this book you've come to realize that flying is within reach. Or better you go fly one time, and I get to hear all about it! You too can become a pilot and create your unexpected adventures.

If you have any other questions (or would like to help me fulfill my lifelong dream of being a passenger in a fighter jet), feel free to email hi@demystiflying.com. I would love to answer any questions you might have. If I don't know the answer, I'll do my best to guide you in the right direction.

Acknowledgements

BEFORE I GET STARTED ON thanking the many individuals that directly contributed to this project, I want to say a few words about writing a book. It's an emotional rollercoaster that makes you question why you said yes to starting the project in the first place. You started swearing off the person who gave you the task to write page after page, only to realize you were the one who assigned yourself this project. Thank you to those, you know who you are, that would watch me love and hate my project days (and even minutes apart).

This was a project that lasted over a few years, and there is no way I would've finished without the help of both the people I consider my dearest. And complete strangers that decided to spend their valuable time answering my many questions. And to all those incredible pilots of history, I never got to meet who put words on paper for me to rediscover so many years later.

Thank you, Lee Abrams, for letting me in on your many wonderful flying adventures.

Thank you, Eskil Amdal, for telling me about your many legendary adventures, including the ability to get into a cockpit after a crash landing, and the importance of nerves.

Thank you, Evan Anderson, for what you've done and for the introductions you provided.

Thank you, Jim Anderson, for answering my email at the very beginning of this project.

Thank you, Erika Armstrong, for being so supportive throughout the project.

Thank you, Brett Balint, for opening the world of the third wave of aviation and giving me an insight into vertical landing aviation.

Thank you, Jim Baird, for talking me through the ups and downs of an airline pilot career.

Thank you, Rob Balzano, for sharing your extensive experience and also for putting smiles on kids through your amazing organization.

Thank you, Tammy Barlette, for sticking it out and doing so inspiring me and so many others.

Thank you, Jamie Beckett, for that much-needed pep talk and for being a wealth of knowledge.

Thank you, Dr. Ing. Gerd Berchtold, for being so passionate about the past, present, and future of aviation.

Thank you, Mark Blois-Brooke, for writing the awesome writeup on LinkedIn and letting me include it in my book.

Thank you, Elizabeth Booker, for sharing your wisdom and so many great books!

Thank you, Mark Brittain, for your friendship and helping me stay on this project before I move onto the next....

Thank you, Randy Brooks, for contagiously sharing your inner passion about the freedom of flying and the work you do to keep pilots safe.

Thank you, Greg Brown, for your colorful description of flying adventures around the globe and for being the best author mentor.

Thank you, Grant C., for sharing your views both as a pilot and flight instructor.

Thank you, Kim "KC" Campbell, for setting the standard for young girls out there.

Thank you, Knight Campbell, for always being so encouraging to me and others and reflecting over your past aviation stories.

Thank you, Ryan Casey, for your thoughtful reflections of your experience.

Thank you, Jeremy Chapman, for telling me about cliff diving in 29 Palms and for the grey school bus reference.

Thank you, Will Chiaffino, for a dream day on the runway and feedback only a future hotshot can give.

Thank you, Sandra Chrystal, for teaching me how to communicate - I'm still a student!

Thank you, Andy Christopher, for taking time multiple times to answer my questions and clarify some of my confusions.

Thank you, Pierre-Henri "ATÉ" Chuet, for having the coolest fighter jet content on YouTube and for sharing your wealth of knowledge with me.

Thank you, Commune, for creating laughters and normality around the table in the weirdest time of our lives.

Thank you, Jessica Cox, for showing the world that everything is possible.

Thank you, Collin Craytor, for always being there to answer any questions and spreading my fondness for small airports.

Thank you, David Culos, for inviting me into the world of aviation and sharing how you seek challenges to always be improving.

Thank you, Warren Curry, for being so frank about your experience and opinions.

Thank you, Dad, for reading every chapter of my first draft and for your continued honesty and excitement.

Thank you, Jeff DeGarmo, for all the introductions that

ended being key to the final result of this book.

Thank you, Susan DeMelo, for being the best listener anyone could ask for.

Thank you, Jason Depew, for being patient with this novice and for writing create content.

Thank you, Peter Docker, for being an intersection of motivation and flying.

Thank you, Genesah Duffy, for being so kind and supportive, hope we get to fly together once!

Thank you, Alaya Dyson, for being so positive about your journey from the cabin to the cockpit - can't wait to be your passenger in the future.

Thank you, Alf Døj, for your honest answers about your pilot journey and for your great sense of humor.

Thank you, Korum Ellis, for sharing your vision for the future of aviation.

Thank you, Lauren Fay, for being the queen of positivity and the one who does it all.

Thank you, Cyndi Finkle, for handstanding your way through the edits.

Thank you, Marcus Forman, for your introductions and positive spirit.

Thank you, James Gentile, for sharing my curiosity and for your introductions.

Thank you, David Gibbons, for being the greatest explainer of aviation training and the adventures that comes with it.

Thank you, Michael Govan, for sharing the beauty of art and aviation with your great stories.

Thank you, Tyler Greenfield, for your constant reminder of how awesome tacos are and continuous support.

Thank you, Tanner Harris, for your contagious enthusiasm and entertaining the similarities between entrepreneurship and aviation.

Thank you, Hazer, for your daily support and the meeting that sparked this project.

Thank you, Louis Heap, for so openly sharing your personal journey and for deciding to bring the joy of flying to others.

Thank you, Tom Heaton, for making me feel better about the project on a daily basis and the introductions.

Thank you, Lorraine M. Herr, for the great chat about airplanes, family, and life.

Thank you, Fiona Hilton Johannessen, for supporting me despite sleepless nights from the very beginning.

Thank you, David Howard, for not standing in the way of me and my McLeod ever again.

Thank you, Erik Huberman, for reporting back about your current training and sharing the joy of soloing.

Thank you, Pauline Hulbert, for telling me about what became one of my favorite books and for giving your perspective from the flight instructor's point of view.

Thank you, Mischa Irsch, for sharing the story about your girls and being so supportive!

Thank you, Tony Kennedy, for coming up with such a creative way for your duaghter to explore "space" and for allowing me to share it with my readers.

Thank you, Jack Kilkeary, for sharing your family story and checking up on my progress.

Thank you, Bjørn Kjos, for telling me about the fighter pilot flying over the Norwegian fields and what was the start of your big aviation adventure.

Thank you, Mike Krass, for writing me back when I first started and connecting me with other pilots and great stories.

Thank you, Mike Krysinski, for the patient walkthrough of the military route while my dog barked non-stop as a helicopter was fittingly circling my house.

Thank you, Kevin Laliberte, for your clarification and nerdy gossip.

Thank you, Katherine Lytton-Foraker, for the unexpected friendship and all the needed nudges.

Thank you, Leo, for being the cutest and most non-contributing co-author in history.

Thank you, Sumner Lee, for sharing incredible stories and pictures of the different aircraft.

Thank you, Travis Ludlow, for showing that age is no barrier for awesome adventures.

Thank you, Nicole Malachowski, for being a trailblazer.

Thank you, Polina Marinova, for showcasing consistency which inspired me through the bumps.

Thank you, Kristin Maryanagam, for providing helpful feedback and being a constant encourager.

Thank you, Florian Masserer, for being a wealth of knowledge of flight school training, especially in Europe, and for checking in on my progress and providing additional information.

Thank you, Johannes Masserer, for the inspiring words and connections from the very beginning of my project.

Thank you, Grace McKellar, for being such a positive spirit and wanting to help others to achieve their pilot dreams.

Thank you, Eric Megerdoomian, for taking the time such a short time before deployment and teaching me the relationship between experience and perceived ability.

Thank you, Jessica Meiris, for passionately teaching me about helicopters.

Thank you, Bryan E. Miller, for a great conversation surrounded by the airport soundtrack.

Thank you, Jarl Mohn, for your continued friendship and many great connections to this project.

Thank you, Mom, for keeping up with my many personalities that shine through when I work on a project and for all the help in shaping this book.

Thank you, Phil McKonkey, for sharing the importance of determination and letting me include your story.

Thank you, Lisa Napoli, for the encouraging email and resources.

Thank you, Zean Nielsen, for being cool despite being Danish and for the introductions.

Thank you, Roger Noble, for your patience, helpful and eloquent explanations.

Thank you, Magnar Nordal, for enthusiastically sharing your knowledge about aviation with me and people all over the world.

Thank you, Miles O'Brien, for being so supportive towards my goal and sharing your own story in such a great storytelling way.

Thank you, Gary Paquette, for giving your unique perspective.

Thank you, Einy Paulsen, for being there for me since day 1 minus two minutes and for being my partner in crime.

Thank you, Helene Pemmer, for reading my many ideas and rants as I was writing this book and for always being there for me.

Thank you, Albert Perez, for sharing your vast experience from the cockpit to the radios and for showing me all your mementos.

Thank you, Bob Pittman, for sharing your story with me and explaining the difference between licenses and ratings to where it finally clicked for me!

Thank you, Sharon Preszler, for inspiring me and others to pursue our dreams and not let barriers stop us.

Thank you, Heather Ramsay, for sending me encouraging words to inspire me on the days it was a little harder to write.

Thank you, Ryan Riley, for the determination you shown from an early age and supporting so many aspects of aviation.

Thank you, Jared Risner, for answering my request for pilots and all my following emails.

Thank you, Vanessa Robaina, for creating the illustrations based on my vision and making me laugh about different heights.

Thank you, Bruce Rose, for sparring on why this book was needed and generously spending your time sharing your experiences.

Thank you, Paige E. Rose, for telling me about your non-traditional path to becoming a helicopter pilot and for supporting me in my journey.

Thank you, Mike Rosenberger, for being a constant cheerleader and recommending some awesome books.

Thank you, Jonathan Rosenthal, for being an incredible storyteller and Swedish banter.

Thank you, Kenyatta Ruffin, for sharing your passion with such energy both on earth and in the skies.

Thank you, Rachel Santana, for encouraging my project sharing your wealth of information, and paving the way for new students.

Thank you, Jan Slangen, for sharing your experiences and journey from surfer dreams to Frecce Tricolori.

Thank you, Dennis Sosa, for brainstorming and pushing me.

Thank you, Charles Stites, for helping so many achieve the dream of flying and for all your help.

Thank you, Beau Suder, for talking me through the cultural differences of aviation and for the continued help beyond the book.

Thank you, Jill Tallman, for picking up the phone and the book recommendations.

Thank you, Sarah Tamar Kohan, for always answering my texts and sharing my love for adventures.

Thank you, Massimo Tammaro, for being an inspiration to me and other student pilots out there!

Thank you, Alexandra Tatarinov, for being the example that when there is a will there is a way and how hard work can help achieve dreams.

Thank you Mike T., for encouraging me to take that first lesson all those years ago.

Thank you, Renaud "Grat" Thys, for answering my many questions in the half-time zone you were in!

Thank you, Alexander Trent, for taking my call during training and sharing your incredible journey across the continents.

Thank you, Carl Valeri, for being so enthusiastic about my project and giving me some great input on my findings.

Thank you, Mike Van Wyk, for sharing how your childhood dream became reality as a pilot on the Fat Albert and inspiring others to fly with air sickness.

Thank you, Mariane Vergassola, for giving your perspective from the other side of the flight cabin.

Thank you, Ariane Virgona, for being the coolest pen pal/ research coach one could ever ask for.

Thank you, Patty Wagstaff, for sharing your story with me.

Thank you, Miles Weidman, for the long text conversation that ended with a brilliant quote.

Thank you, Michael Wildes, for being a friend in this journey and for sharing your passion for aviation with me and the world.

Thank you, Ray Wilson, for sharing your dad's story and protecting our streets.

Thank you, Jessica Wolcott, for giving me an insight into the world of an airline pilot and your journey of getting there.

ACKNOWLEDGEMENTS

And to all the people that have positively impacted me on the path, thank you from the bottom of my heart.

About the author

KINE A. PAULSEN IS A corporate advisor, investor, and a student pilot. She is also co-author of *The Life of Twins: Insights from over 120 twins, friends, and family*. She resides in Los Angeles.